TELL ME
MORE ABOUT
INDIA

SWARN KHANDPUR

INDIA BOOK HOUSE LIMITED

ISBN 81-85028-54-0
© Swarn Khandpur 1994, 2000
Cover design and illustrations : Pradeep Sathe

Published by
INDIA BOOK HOUSE LIMITED
412, Tulsiani Chambers,
Nariman Point,
Mumbai – 400 021.

Printed at
Krishna Art Printery Pvt. Ltd.,
Byculla (E),
Mumbai – 400 027.

CONTENTS

"If there is one place on the face of the earth where all the dreams of living men have found a home from the very earliest days when man began the dream of existence, it is India."

— **Romain Rolland**

ARCHITECTURE

Why is India called the 'land of temples' ?

The practice of building temples in stone and brick began about 1,500 years ago. The earlier wooden sanctuaries enshrining the images of the Hindu Gods, Jain Tirthankaras and Buddhist symbols were gradually replaced by stone temples. In course of time, temples sprang up all over India, and to build a temple or to donate gifts for its benefit were considered meritorious acts. Between 900 and 1,600 A.D., thousands of imposing temples with beautiful carvings were built. The temple craftsmanship evoked universal admiration and the remark that "Indians built like titans and finished like jewellers"!

The temple became the hub of all activity. Towns and cities evolved round the temple which was maintained by grants donated by kings and chiefs, and offerings made by devotees. Music and dance recitals were dedicated to the deity. Artisans flourished because of the demand for their crafts. Often the temple maintained schools and served as a hostel for travellers. The temple, therefore, was not merely a place of worship, it was the centre of all social and cultural life.

With the advent of Christianity, Islam and Sikhism, churches, mosques and gurdwaras also sprang up side by side with temples. Frequent invasions of north India destroyed several temples; the south luckily escaped the onslaught. Still, India is dotted with thousands of temples, though some of them are now in ruins.

Why were temples dedicated to the Sun God ?

Surya, the Sun God, is the source of light and life. He is also considered to be a great healer of skin diseases. Therefore, in olden days, temples and pools were built to the Sun for religious and medicinal reasons.

During the Vedic times, Surya was worshipped only through chants and rituals. In fact, the *Gayatri Mantra,* one of the most sacred hymns in the *Vedas*, was chanted both at dawn and dusk, facing the Sun. *Surya Namaskar* was an ancient *yogic* exercise performed by exposing the bare body to the rays of the morning Sun.

Earlier, there were no idols of the Sun or temples. The practice of making idols began with the advance of the Greeks, Persians and Shakas. The foreign influence is evident in the earlier idols depicted with a long coat, trousers and boots. It was only from the 4th century A.D., that the idols assumed Indian clothes, and temples to the Sun God sprang up everywhere.

The largest and most famous of the Sun temples is the Konarak temple of Orissa, built by King Narasimha Deva in the 13th century. It was in the shape of a gigantic chariot with 24 sculptured wheels and seven stone horses straining to pull the chariot. Although in ruins, it still stands in testimony to its past glory.

The Sun temple of Kashmir, built in the 8th century by King Lalitaditya, was named the Martand temple after one of Surya's epithets. The Modhera Sun temple in Gujarat was built in the 11th century. The Solanki rulers were lavish in its construction. Even in decay, the temple possesses a rare grandeur.

All Sun temples were constructed in such a way that the first rays of the rising Sun fell on the altar.

When the practice of Sun worship declined, the Sun temples were neglected. Now in ruins, they once stood majestic, basking in the blazing glory of their deity.

How was the Great Temple built ?

The Great Temple, also called the Brihadeshwara temple, at Thanjavur, in Tamil Nadu, is one of the most spectacular temples of south India. It was the first temple to be built of large granite stone blocks, rising to an enormous height of 66 m. About a thousand years ago when it was built, no cementing mixture was used. The builders relied only on the downward pressure of one stone placed exactly upon another to keep them in place – an extremely difficult task!

Look at the huge rounded stone which forms the top of the temple. It is a single massive block and weighs 80 tonnes! How did the builders manage to hoist it to that height at a time when modern mechanical aids like cranes were unknown?

9

Well,they built a sloping ramp of mud 6 kms away from the temple, gradually rising to the height of 6 m, the highest point of the temple. Very gradually, with great effort, the huge stone was dragged up to the top to its crowning position.

This Shiva temple decorated with beautiful carved figures, recalls the might of its royal builder, the Chola King, Rajaraja the Great.

Built about the same time are the beautiful set of temples at Khajuraho in Madhya Pradesh and the magnificent Lingaraja Temple at Bhubaneshwar, Orissa.
You may see a marked difference in the styles of temple towers of the north from those of the south.

In the north, the tower usually has a rounded top and a curvilinear outline ...

... while the tower of the south is usually in the shape of a truncated pyramid.

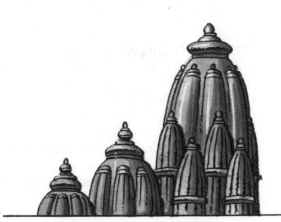

What were 'cave temples'?

A 'cave temple' was a novel type of architecture. Caves were excavated from a hill for shrines and dwellings where monks could spend their time in scholarly seclusion. This rock-cut architecture developed in size and splendour with over 1,200 rock-excavations being executed in parts of northern, eastern and western India and the Deccan. Not only Buddhists, but Jains and Hindus freely took to rock-cut architecture to find lasting abodes for their gods.

Look at the interior of the cave at Karla, near Bombay.

The Ajanta caves have become famous the world over for their exquisite frescoes depicting the stories of Buddha.

Excavated 1,900 years ago, the cave was cut 124 ft. deep into the rock with pillars of similar height.

The masterpieces of rock-architecture are at Ajanta and Ellora in Maharashtra.

One of the most amazing of the Hindu caves is the Kailasa temple at Ellora. It is carved out of a single rock which was excavated by digging a deep three-sided trench from above, leaving the block of rock for the temple in the centre. Then starting from the top, the temple was carved, complete with the main shrine, the entrance gate, a smaller shrine for Nandi (the mount of Shiva) and a hall surrounded by pillars. The whole temple is sculptured with stories from the epics. The temple, built by the Rashtrakuta dynasty, took 100 years to complete, more than a thousand years ago.

What is a stepwell ?

A stepwell, like any other well, is a source of water, but has an unusual design.

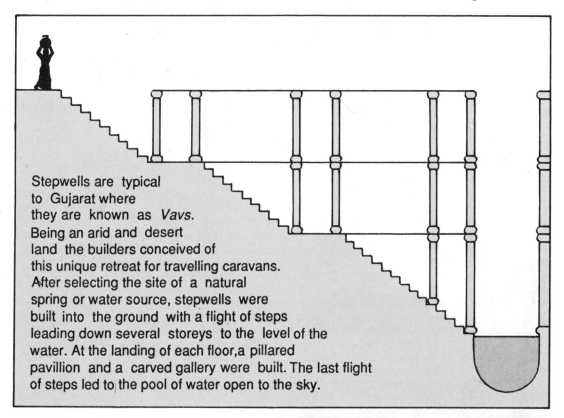

Stepwells are typical to Gujarat where they are known as *Vavs*. Being an arid and desert land the builders conceived of this unique retreat for travelling caravans. After selecting the site of a natural spring or water source, stepwells were built into the ground with a flight of steps leading down several storeys to the level of the water. At the landing of each floor, a pillared pavillion and a carved gallery were built. The last flight of steps led to the pool of water open to the sky.

As stepwells were incredibly cool, they became the meeting place for communities as well. Both Hindu and Muslim chiefs of Gujarat patronised constructions of such wells. The earliest built stepwell dates back to the 7th century and the last one was probably built sometime in the 1930s.

Most of the stepwells are found in Saurashtra. The one at Adalaj, 2 kms north of Ahmedabad, has five storeys. The walls have carved niches, panels and the image of Goddess Durga to whom the well was dedicated.

Most of the stepwells have now dried up. But they remain silent testimonials to the engineering and hydraulics knowledge of a bygone era.

Where are square, rectangular or circular temples found ?

A typical Kerala temple can be square, rectangular or circular in shape.

If the temple is circular, the roof resembles a big cone ...

... if square, the roof is pyramidal ...

... and if it is rectangular, the roof will be ridged.

Great attention is paid to the construction of these roofs. This type of temple architecture is unique to Kerala. Due to the heavy monsoon here, the roofs are generally covered with tiles. Moreover, the profuse use of wood in both art and architecture has lent an elegance to their designs.

Where are the 'Shaking Minars' ?

The mosque of
Siddi Bashir at Ahmedabad
has 'shaking minars' on
either side of its main entrance.
A flat terrace joins the two
minars (minarets), serving as
a bridge. Each minar is more
than 20 m high and has
three storeys with carved
balconies. They are designed in
such a way that when
the top portion of one minar is
moved, the vibrations pass
to the other, which responds
in movement.

These minars are
shaken many times a
day for the benefit
of visitors who climb to the top
to watch them move. As one
minar starts swinging back
and forth, the other,
some distance away, also
sways rhythmically.
These 'shaking minars',
built 400 years ago,
are an architectural and
engineering wonder.

Which monument takes on different hues with every change of light ?

The world-famous Taj Mahal at Agra assumes different hues according to the light that encompasses it. This dream monument changes from a soft cream at dawn to a dazzling white at midday, to a gentle pink at sunset and a silvery white by moonlight.

Built by the Mughal Emperor Shah Jahan as a mausoleum for his beloved wife Mumtaz Mahal, the Taj Mahal took 22 years and 20,000 men to complete.

The delicate inlay work on the white marble has given colour and design to the monument. About 43 different types of gems such as the yellow topaz, deep red garnet, brown and grey onyx, deep blue sapphire, bright red carnelian, green jade of China, turquoise of Tibet and precious blue lapis lazuli of Afghanistan, have been embedded into carefully cut patterns in the marble.

This magnificent monument is counted among the wonders of the medieval world.

Which mausoleum has the largest dome in India ?

The Gol Gumbaz at Bijapur, Karnataka, has the distinction of being one of the largest round domes in the world, second only to St. Peter's dome in Rome.

Built in the complex of tombs of the Adil Shah Sultans, the dome measures 42 m in diameter and is unsupported by pillars.

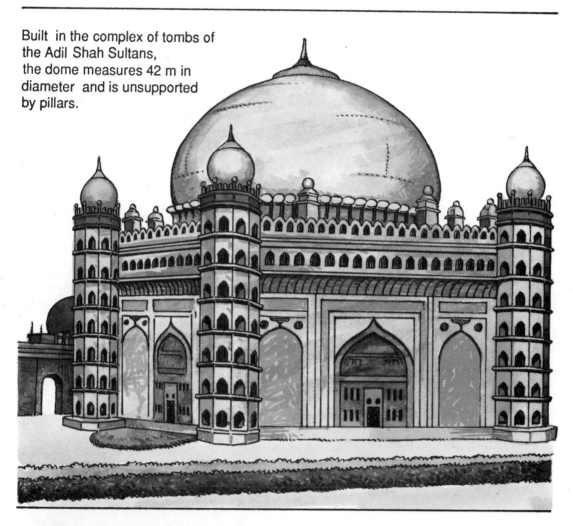

All round inside the dome is a broad gallery, the entrance to which is through corner towers. Inside, one can experience extraordinary sound effects – the lighting of a matchstick, the rustling of paper, even a whisper at one point of the gallery is magnified and heard most distinctly at the opposite end. No wonder it is called the 'Whispering Gallery' of the Gol Gumbaz.

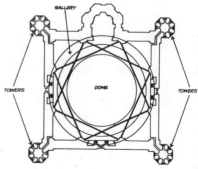

Which place in India built houses in wood till the 19th century ?

Hundreds of years ago, when India was thickly forested, houses were built in wood. But wood being a perishable material, most of the houses are no more. Yet, in Gujarat, the use of wood in architecture survived till the 19th century, and there remains some rare old houses mainly made of wood and decorated with wood-carvings.

In one of the few surviving *havelis,* there are wooden columns, balconies, ceilings and even wooden weather shades. The latches and bolts to secure doors are also designed in wood. And they are all exquisitely carved! The best carving designs appear on the entrance doorways which are considered auspicious by the Gujaratis.

Wooden architecture is a very ancient art. And the technique of this art was, to some extent, repeated in medieval stone temples where stone imitated woodwork in its forms.

Have you ever seen houses built on stilts? Well, in some parts of India, for example in some north-eastern states and in the Nicobar Islands, people build houses on stilts because of heavy rains. Although not easy to build, these houses with wooden frames and thatched roofs, look very attractive.

SCIENCE

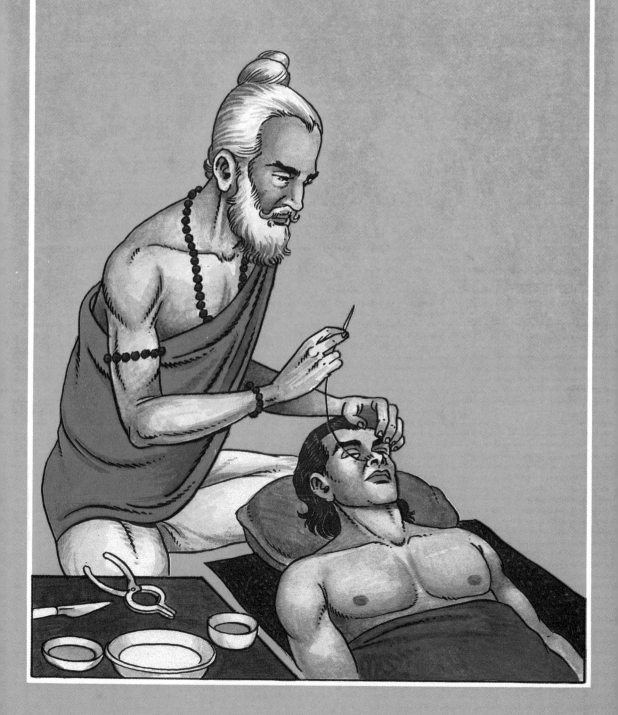

Which gift was given to Alexander by Porus?

The gift was not gold or silver but thirty pounds of steel made in India! This rare gift was presented to Alexander the Great in 326 B.C. – more than 2,000 years ago.

The making of steel, which is basically an alloy of iron and carbon, was a village craft. Indian smiths were the first in the world to manufacture steel. In fact, it was exported way back between 700 and 800 B.C! Indian steel was highly valued all over the world and came to be called 'wootz'. Steel swords by Indian craftsmen were highly prized.

In the 19th century, Europe discovered processes which revolutionised steel-making. In India, Jamshedji N.Tata turned a village craft into an industry by establishing the first iron and steel mill at Jamshedpur (Bihar) in 1907. He is thus known as the 'Father of the Steel Industry' in India.

Which are the marvels of ancient India?

As far back as 2,000 years ago, Indians had reached a very high standard in stone carving. The Ashokan pillars of India, were carved from single blocks of stone . Some of them are 14 m high, surmounted with finely carved capitals. One such capital – the Lion capital from Sarnath – has been adopted as India's state emblem.

These pillars display a mastery over material. Though made of sandstone, they shine as if they are made of brass! Strangely, this high polish technique was never again used in Indian sculpture.

More remarkable is the Iron Pillar at Delhi. Made of a single piece of iron, 7.32 m in length, the pillar tapers down from a base of 40 cm to 30 cm at the top . It weighs about 6 tonnes. Although standing for nearly 1600 years, it has remained rust free till today. A pillar of such size and weight could not have been produced by the best European foundaries until about a century ago.

Another proof of the metallurgical skill of ancient India is the copper statue of the Buddha found in Sultanganj (Bihar). This graceful figure is over 2.13 m in height and weighs nearly a tonne. It may interest you to know that copper was the first metal to be used in India. Copper deposits are found only at Khetri in Rajasthan.

Which Indian concepts in mathematics have led to present-day developments in science and technology?

Indian mathematicians have given to the world zero; the numbers, namely 1,2,3, to 9; and 'position value notation'. Most of the great discoveries and inventions of which the west is so proud would have been impossible without these concepts.

Zero, in ancient India, was represented as a circle with a dot at its centre, and was called *shoonya.* As it travelled to distant lands, it acquired different names until it came to be called 'zero'.

Zero does not mean 'nothing'; it is a number. Bhaskara, an ancient Indian mathematician claimed that any number divided by zero is infinity. Zero led to thinking of numbers less than zero itself.

Further, to write big numbers, the Indians developed the system of fixing places for units, tens, hundreds etc., which is called 'position value notation' today. In this way, the position of a digit in a number determines its value e.g. (1992=1x10x10x10+9x10x10+9x10+2).

Thus Indians could write big numbers while Romans with their number system consisting of M's and C's could not count beyond a particular number.

For many years it was thought that the Indian numbers including zero, were invented by the Arabs. In Europe, they were even called 'Arabic numbers' for quite some time, for the Arabs, after learning these from India, spread them to Europe.

Why was India's first satellite named 'Aryabhata'?

Aryabhata was the first of the great astronomers and mathematicians of ancient India. Many of his theories and calculations which he recorded in his book *Aryabhatiya* are valued even today. To honour this great Indian, India's first satellite was named after him.

Aryabhata was the first to deduce that the earth is round and revolves around the sun; that the earth rotates on its axis, thus creating day and night of 23 hrs. 56 min. and 4.1 sec. – almost equivalent to present-day calculations; also that solar and lunar eclipses occur because of the shadows cast by the earth and the moon.

In mathematics, he was the first to approximate the value of pi to 3.1416 which is accepted today.

What is the 'science of longevity' called?

Ayurveda, which literally means the 'science of life', is an ancient healing system of medicine. It forms a part of the *Atharva Veda,* one of the four *Vedas* of the Hindus. It is said that Lord Brahma himself unfolded this knowledge to sage Atreya, who is known as the first teacher of Ayurveda.

According to Ayurveda, health is maintained through the even balance of the three vital fluids of the body - wind, bile (gall) and phlegm. Illness is caused when the balance among these three is disturbed. Herbs and therapies form part of the treatment but great emphasis is laid on preventive measures. A balanced life style, in short, leads to a healthy body. Ayurveda lost its popularity with the advent of the modern system of allopathy. Once again, the Ayurvedic system of medicine is being revived. The National Institute of Ayurveda at Jaipur; Gujarat Ayurveda University at Jamnagar; and Department of Ayurveda in the Benaras Hindu University at Varanasi are the premier institutes engaged in training, teaching, research and cure in Ayurveda.

Which ancient text contains an oath of honesty and service to mankind similar to the Hippocrates oath?

The Ayurvedic treaties, *Charakasamhita,* written by Charaka in the first century A.D. contains an oath similar to the Hippocrates oath which is administered to medical graduates of modern times.

Charaka, in his treaties, enumerates a large number of diseases and gives methods for their diagnosis and treatment. He also mentions the secretion of gastric juice and its role in digestion, long before modern physicians discovered this fact. That is not all. He even lays down rules of professional behaviour which were told to students at a solemn ceremony, on the completion of their studies. These rules remind us of the Hippocrates oath and are worthy of any conscientious doctor of any time.

What is Varahamihira's contribution to hydrology?

Varahamihira, a scientist of the 6th century, made a significant observation that the presence of a termite colony indicates an underground source of water nearby. His claim is gaining prominence in the scientific world today.

He was also the first to claim that some 'force' might be keeping bodies stuck to the earth. Interestingly, the force is now called 'gravity'.

Who introduced plastic surgery in India?

Sushruta, a surgeon of the 6th century B.C. practised rhinoplasty 2,600 years ago in India! His technique inspired the surgeons of the East India Company who used it and thus rhinoplasty was introduced to the world in the 18th century. No wonder, Sushruta is called the father of plastic surgery in the world.

Sushruta was the son of the *vedic* sage, Vishvamitra and student of Dhanvantari of Kashi (Varanasi). His treatise, *Sushrutasamhita* is an encyclopaedia of medical science with special emphasis on surgery.

Sushruta advocated what is today called the 'caesarean' operation. An expert in removing stones from the bladder, locating and treating fractures and doing eye operations for cataract, he could also repair noses, ears and lips lost or injured in battle or cut as a punishment for adultery or robbery. He would administer wine to patients before the operation as a form of anaesthesia! His names for the instruments based on the birds or animals they resemble, for example, crocodile forceps and hawkbill forceps are adopted even today.

Which Mughal Emperor was a naturalist?

Emperor Jahangir was a keen observer of birds, animals and plants. His memoirs contain the various characteristics of animals and birds, their geographical distribution and behaviour.

Jahangir had a zoo where he would watch birds. His observation about sarus cranes – how they mate and brood; their love for each other and for their eggs, is remarkable. His estimate of the gestation period of elephants of 18 to 19 months was proved correct by zoologists nearly 200 years later! He was responsible for the cultivation of high altitude trees such as cypress, juniper and pine on the plains.

Jahangir's collection of paintings of rare animals, birds and plants, is remarkable. The discovery of the portrait of a Mauritius dodo – a large, non-flying pigeon-like bird that was presented to him around 1624 created a sensation in the world of ornithology. This bird had become extinct about 300 years ago !

When were rockets first used for military purpose?

The Sultans of Mysore, Haider Ali and Tipu Sultan were the first in the world to make use of rockets against the British army.

In the battle of Pollilur on September 10, 1780, Tipu Sultan used rockets and set fire to the carriage carrying British ammunitions. These iron-encased rockets tied to bamboo poles, with a range of upto 3 kms, caused considerable panic and confusion in the enemy ranks. The British lost the battle and regarded it as the 'severest blow to them ever sustained in India'.

The battle of Pollilur has been depicted in a long mural at the Darya Daulat Palace at Srirangapattinam, the island capital of erstwhile Mysore State.

After Tipu's death, the British appropriated the rocket technology and developed it further. Thereafter rockets became a part of armoury in subsequent warfare.

Two hundred years later, in 1988, India successfully fired its first surface to surface missile, *Prithvi*, not against any enemy, but to test the country's skill in this technology !

What is Jantar Mantar?

Jantar Mantar is the distorted form of the Sanskrit words *Yantra Mantra* which mean instrument and formula. Sawai Jai Singh II (1686-1743), the King of Amber in Rajasthan, built big observatories in stone at Delhi, Jaipur, Ujjain, Varanasi and Mathura to probe the mysteries of the heavens with the unaided human eye. These observatories have come to be known as Jantar Mantars. At present, the observatories at Ujjain and Varanasi are in ruins and the one at Mathura no longer exists.

What is Samrat Yantra?

The Samrat Yantra is a sundial which shows local solar time accurate to half a minute !

The Samrat Yantra is located in the observatory at Jaipur.

Designed by Sawai Jai Singh more than 250 years ago, in stone and plaster, it measures time, and determines the altitude of the sun.
It is the biggest sundial in the world.

The Ram Yantra is another instrument that locates the positions of various heavenly bodies.

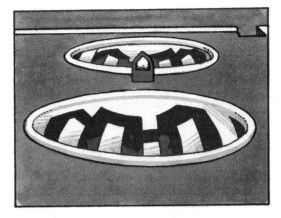

The Jai Prakash, another instrument in the shape of a wide concave bowl, maps out the positions of all heavenly bodies round the clock.

Jai Singh's achievements in science are remarkable. Without the help of the telescope, he could detect the errors in the findings of European astronomers. Instead of the small brass instruments huge masonry structures – perhaps to huge masonry structures - perphaps to popularise astronomy among the masses.

What is Yoga ?

The word *yoga* is derived from the Sanskrit root *yuj,* meaning 'to join' or 'to unite'. *Yoga* is the technique prescribed by Patanjali, a great philosopher of ancient India, to reach higher levels of consciousness by proper training of the mind and body. Thus *yoga* is both a system of philosophy for spiritual advancement as well as a complete science for physical and mental health.

The popular concept of *yoga* particularly in the West, is of certain postures (*asanas*) and exercises such as breath control (*pranayama*) only. In fact these are only two of the eight disciplines of training in *yoga*. Once all eight are mastered, it enables one to hold one's breath for extended periods without suffering injury; control the rhythm of one's own heart-beat; withstand extremes of heat and cold; remain healthy on a meagre diet and survive to an advanced age without impairment of one's faculties.

The earliest evidence of *yoga* is found in the stone seals discovered at the Harappan excavation sites.

Shirshasana
or
Head-Stand

Trikonasana
or
Triangle Posture

Bhunjangasana
or
the Cobra Position

SPORTS

Which is the oldest sport in India ?

Wrestling.

Indian mythology is full of colourful tales of wrestling bouts of heroes such as Balarama, Sugriva, Ravana and several others. Hanuman the monkey-god is worshipped by wrestlers even today, as a symbol of strength.

With the coming of the Mughals, the golden age of wrestling began. They patronised this sport and spent money on the training and upkeep of wrestlers. Tournaments were held and the successful wrestler was honoured with the title of Rustam-e-Hind and a silver mace.

Perhaps the most famous of Indian wrestlers was Ghulam. He was sent to Paris in 1900 by Moti Lal Nehru where he grappled with the world-famous wrestler of Turkey and won. After Ghulam's death, three new wrestlers named Ghulam came forward but the Ghulam of Datia rose to eminence. Lovingly called Gama, he remained unbeaten in his career. He even received the Champion's John Bull Belt in London by pinning down wrestlers of other countries.

Wrestling later became a neglected sport till it was revived as a sports event in the Olympics.

Which present-day international sport originated in Kerala ?

Karate, a popular international sport these days, had its origin in India. *Kalarippayattu* or simply *payattu,* is one of the martial exercises practised in Kerala. It is a combat technique for self-defence.

In the 2nd century, a Buddhist monk from India named Bodhidharma went to China to teach at a monastery. To his dismay, he found that his student-monks were timid and weak. To improve their vitality, Bodhidharma taught *pranayam* (breathing exercises) and exercises in self-defence. These exercises became very popular in China and gradually Kempo, the Chinese form of Karate, developed. From China, it spread to Japan, where it developed into its present form, Karate literally means 'empty hand' fighting. Anyone who practises karate is called *Karateka*.

Which Indian sport is similar to gymnastics ?

Mallakhamb literally means 'gymnast's pole'. The sport involves controlling one's body round a smooth pole fixed to the ground, to strengthen the muscles.

Mallakhamb was first mentioned in a 12th century classic *Manasolhas* of south India. However, the sport was revived by the physical instructor of Peshwa Baji Rao II, only about 200 years ago. Maratha soldiers were particularly expert in Mallakhamb.

It has now evolved into a fascinating sport and several new variations have been added. Mallakhamb is one of the 15 disciplines in Bharatiyam, the Indian extravaganza being popularised by the government.

For which sport is the Ekalavya award instituted ?

The Ekalavya award is presented to the best player in Kho Kho. As the game is played by women also, the best woman player is awarded the Rani Laxmi award.

Kho Kho is essentially an Indian game. Indian mythology mentions that Lord Krishna used to play a similar game with his friends in Brindavan. Kho Kho was once called *rathera* because it was played on *raths* (chariots) and this form was much patronised by the Chalukyas and Rashtrakutas of the Deccan around the 9th century. It is one of the popular sports of Maharashtra; in fact, the word *'kho'* in Marathi means 'go and chase'.

Kho Kho was a demonstration game in the 1982 Asian Games at Delhi, and also in the 1987 South Asian Federation Games at Calcutta.

By what other names is Kabaddi known in India ?

Kabaddi, like Kho Kho, is a typically Indian game. It has been played as *hu-tu-tu* in Maharashtra, *do-do-do* in Bengal and *chedu-gudu* in the south.

Kabaddi is a robust sport and has a popular appeal. This seven-a-side sport, played by both men and women, does not require any special gear or outfit. It is played on a court, marked out on soft ground, and divided into two halves. The aim is to cross over to the opponent's court, one player at a time, and to touch one of the opponents. The most important requisite is that the invading player has to utter a chant holding his breath till he returns to the safety of his own court without being caught. If he returns without touching anyone but holding onto his chant, neither side loses a player.

Kabaddi has many forms but the Sanjeevani style has been officially recognised. In this form, a player, once out, can be revived, when an opponent is out. Usually the sport consists of two sessions of 20 minutes each.

Which ancient Indian game was the forerunner of the modern game of Chess ?

The Indian game of Chaturanga is now known as Chess.

Chaturanga, meaning 'four parts', was a war game comprising elephants, horses, chariots and foot soldiers.

Chaturanga spread to Persia and Arabia. The Arabs called it *Shatranj.* It reached Europe by the 10th century where it became Chess. The name 'Chess' comes from the Persian word *Shah,* meaning a 'king' or 'ruler'. The term checkmate is *shahmat* in Persian meaning 'the king is dead'.

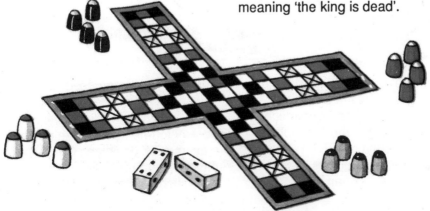

Today chess is a competitive sport that requires immense concentration, skill and wisdom. Viswanathan Anand, a prodigy in chess, has brought glory to India by becoming India's first grandmaster at the age of eighteen.

What is the ancient game of 'stick-and-ball' called today ?

The ancient game of 'stick-and-ball' played nearly 4,000 years ago, is known today as 'hockey'. The word 'hockey' appears to have come into general use sometime during the 19th century.

While it is difficult to state when and where hockey was first played, history confirms that early man carrying a club, staff or stick, must have hit at moveable objects by instinct. In India, a game resembling hockey was popular. It was called by different local names, one of which was *khiddo-khundi* meaning 'cotton ball and twisted stick'.

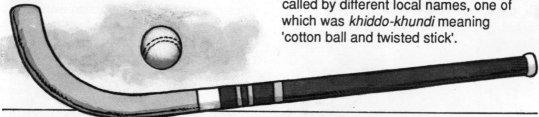

Modern hockey evolved in England and was brought to India by the British. The game soon caught the imagination of the Indian people and the first club was formed in Calcutta in 1885. Within ten years, famous competitions like the Beighton Cup and Aga Khan

Tournament commenced. At the Olympic Games between 1928 and 1956, Indian teams won every single hockey tournament. Some of the great players such as Dhyan Chand became national heroes. Hockey is regarded as the national game of India.

Where was the first polo club established in India ?

The Calcutta Polo Club is the oldest 'recognised' polo club in the world.

Polo is a very ancient sport. After the domestication of horses by the Iranian tribes, cavalry units became the backbone of their fighting forces, and this sport was invented to keep the men in shape.

Polo derives its name from *pulu*, the Tibetan word meaning a ball. The game was brought to India by the Muslim conquerors where it flourished under the name of *chaugan*. It is said that Qutubuddin, the first Sultan of Delhi, died of injuries when he fell off his horse while playing *chaugan*. The Mughal Emperor Akbar was particularly fond of this game and is credited with framing rules for the game. He even played it at night with lighted balls.

Polo spread to other countries but interest in the game gradually waned in India except in areas like Giligir and Manipur where it was played by people in its original form on small local ponies British planters in north-east India found the sport interesting and started playing it. From them, it was passed on to the British soldiers who established polo clubs all over the country, the Calcutta Polo Club being the first among them.

Polo tournaments are held in India and the Bangalore Polo Trophy is considered to be the largest trophy in the world.

Polo is an expensive game as only the rich can afford to maintain horses. That is why it is called the 'game of princes'. Many of the terms used in polo originate from Indian words. Each seven-minute period of the game is called a 'Chukka', and the riding breeches worn by the players are called 'jodhpurs', after a city in Rajasthan.

In 1976, a polo match was organised at Jaipur in which the players were mounted on elephants instead of horses. The sport became so popular that a 'World Elephant Polo Tournament' was held in 1982 for the first time.

Where is the Patang (Kite) Museum located in India ?

The Patang Museum, located at Ahmedabad (Gujarat), is one of the only two kite museums in the world, the other one being in Tokyo.

Set up in 1986 with the collection of Shri Bhanu Shah, the Kite Museum's director, the museum has more than 1,500 brightly coloured kites in myriad shapes and sizes. There is one kite made of more than 450 pieces of paper! And among others, is a kite nearly 100 years old. The unique feature of the museum is that no kite is painted.

Along with the kites, the making of *manja* (sturdy thread needed to fly the kite) is also demonstrated by the craftsmen in the museum.

Where is the international kite-flying fete held in India ?

For three days in January, Ahmedabad's skyline becomes a riot of colour as kites of all shapes, sizes and hues zig-zag across the blue of the sky. Champion kite-fliers from different parts of India compete with those from other countries, while thousands of spectators cheer the participants on. A wide range of prizes in cash and kind are offered to the winners.

It is believed that kite-making originated in China more than 2,500 years ago. Kites entered India with the Mughals or perhaps with the Chinese traders. Gradually kite-flying became a popular sport almost all over India. In Gujarat it has become a part of the *Makar*

Sankranti (January 14) festival which is celebrated to mark the end of winter. Throughout the state, the festival is celebrated with kite-flying and feasting.

By arranging the international kite-flying fete at Ahmedabad, the Government of Gujarat has given a new dimension to local celebrations.

Who is regarded as the greatest long distance swimmer in the world ?

Mihir Sen has been acknowledged in the *Guinness Book of Records* as the greatest long distance swimmer.

Mihir Sen is the only swimmer in the world, to date, to swim several straits in one calendar year (1966).
He crossed the Palk Straits between India and Sri Lanka in April; the shark-infested Straits of Gilbraltar between Europe and Africa in August; the Dardanelles (Turkey) on September 12 and the Bosphorous, nine days later on September 21. His tryst with the Pacific started on October 29. He swam the 85 kms long Panama Canal in about 34 hours, thus setting the world's fastest record. Mihir was also the first Indian to swim the English Channel way back in 1958.

In recent years, swimming has become an adventure sport. Swimming across the Channel and different straits has become popular. Taranath Shenoy who is deaf and dumb, swam across the Straits of Gibraltar, thus becoming the first handicapped swimmer to do so. Arti Shah became the first Indian woman to swim the English Channel in 1959.

Which international games were either invented or evolved in India ?

Snooker and badminton.

Snooker was invented in 1875 in Jabalpur by Colonel N.F. Chamberlain, who was bored with playing billiards. The various colours of the balls made snooker very popular and tournaments were held regularly at Ootacamund in southern India, before it reached England in 1885.

Geet Sethi has been India's best snooker player to date.

Badminton, on the other hand, is believed to have evolved in Pune as the first laws of the game were drawn up there in mid 1870's. The game was therefore called 'poona' for some time before it got its modern name . Prakash Padukone has won more national and international titles than any other Indian badminton player.

Why were the famous Bombay Pentangular Cricket Tournaments stopped ?

The Pentangular Cricket Tournaments ended in 1945 when Mahatma Gandhi agitated against them for being communal in character.

Cricket was brought to India by the British. It was first played at Cambay by

the merchants of the East India Company, who also started the Calcutta Cricket Club at the Eden Gardens. The sport remained localised among the British till they played a match with a Parsi team in 1892. The tournament became triangular, with the Hindus fielding a team and then quadrangular with the entry of Muslims. A fifth team, the Rest, was added and the tournaments became pentangular. These tournaments stopped in 1945 following Mahatma Gandhi's agitation against them.

Today cricket is the most popular sport in the country. On an average, a cricket match may attract a crowd of at least 50,000 persons. During international matches, thousands of people tune in to radio sets or watch 'live' telecasts.

Even women are greatly interested in the sport. It is said that an Australian school teacher first introduced cricket among her girl students at Kottayam (Kerala) in 1913. The Indian Women's Cricket Association was formed in 1973.

India also boasts of having the highest cricket ground in the world. It is at Chail at an altitude of 2,250 m, forty-five kms. from Shimla.

After whom is the national championship for cricket named ?

Ranji Trophy, the national cricket championship, is named after the famous cricketer, K.S. Ranjitsinhji, the Maharaja Jam Sahib of Nawanagar (1872-1933).

Ranjitsinhji, fondly called Ranji, had little cricket background when he went to England for further studies. But he soon developed his abilities and set many batting records. In 1899, he became the first batsman in England to score 3,000 runs in a season.

The Ranji Trophy was instituted in 1934 in memory of Ranjitsinhji by the Board of Control for Cricket in India (formed in 1927). It has been contested annually ever since without interruption. The various state associations in the five zones – North, West, South, East and Central – participate in the zonal championships. Bombay has won the Ranji Trophy the maximum number of times.

Over the years, the Ranji Trophy matches have become the basis of selection for the national cricket team. India today is one of the nine leading cricket playing countries in the world, with several distinguished cricketers, like Vijay Hazare, Vijay Merchant, Vinoo Mankad, Sunil Gavaskar, and Kapil Dev.

In which sport does the 'gold' score nine points ?

In the modern sport of target archery (toxophily), the archer scores nine points when his arrow hits the 'gold', which is the innermost of the five concentric circles of different colours. These circles of gold, red, blue, black and white carry 9, 7, 5, 3 and 1 points respectively.

Archery has been used for hunting and self-defence since 8000 B.C. In some parts of India, the tribals still use bow and arrow to hunt animals.

The bow and arrow were among the earliest weapons of warfare. In ancient India archery contests were a popular pastime of the warrior class. There are several outstanding archery feats mentioned in our scriptures. Rama, the hero of *Ramayana* won the hand of Sita, at a great archery contest. Arjuna, the Pandava warrior of the *Mahabharata* exhibited his skill in archery by shooting a revolving fish in the eye by looking at its reflection in a cauldron of boiling oil.

With the decline of the bow as a weapon of warfare, the art of bowmanship greatly lost its appeal. It has been revived as a sport and was included in the 1972 Olympic Games. The original bamboo bows and arrows have been replaced by fibre glass bows and aluminium arrows. As a result, the equipment is cost-intensive and archery has become an expensive sport.

At Beijing, in 1972 India's best known archers, Limba Ram, Shyam Lal and Dorji, won the 'Asia Cup' in archery. Significantly, all three archers are of tribal origin.

Tir meaning 'arrow' is still the traditional betting game of the tribals of Meghalaya.

PERFORMING ARTS

By what name is Tanna Mishra better known in the world of music?

Tanna Mishra, the son of a village priest near Gwalior was renowned as the famous Tansen or 'Master of Musical Notes'. This name was given to him by Raja Vikramjit of Gwalior. Tansen later converted to Islam and was known as Miyan Tansen.

According to a legend, Tansen as a child is believed to have startled Swami

Haridas, a saint singer of Vrindavan, by roaring like a lion. Impressed with the child's voice, the Swami took him under his tutelage and rigorously trained him as a singer.

Patronized by several kings, Tansen's career culminated at the court of the great Mughal Akbar, where he became one of the 'Nine Gems' in the group of talented men.

Tansen was an accomplished singer of the *dhrupad*. He was also the creator of new *ragas* eventually named after him like *Miyan ki Malhar* and *Miyan ki Todi*. Legend has it that he set unlit lamps ablaze when he sang *raga Deepak*. To cool down the immense heat thus generated, his daughter sang *raga Malhar* and invoked rain as an antidote. He is also believed to have written scholarly treatises on the *dhrupada raga* in pristine form, and on Hindustani musical tradition.

Tansen lies buried near Mohammad Ghouse's tomb at Gwalior (Ghouse was also his music teacher). His legacy survives to this day. Every year, musicians gather at his tomb for the Tansen Samaroh.

What are the basic elements of Indian music?

The *raga* (melody), *bhava* (emotions) and *tala* (rhythmic beat) form the basic components of Indian music.

The word *raga* is derived from the Sanskrit word *ranj* which means,

'to please'. There are several hundred *ragas* but six *ragas* (Bhairav, Kausika, Hindola, Dipaka, Sriraga and Megha) are considered to be the main ones. *Raga Bhairavi* is deemed to be the *adi* or the first *raga*.

Each of the six *ragas* is generally supposed to have 'wives' or *raginis* and a number of offspring.

Further, each *raga* and *ragini* is assigned to a particular time of day or night and is associated with a particular *bhava.* For example, *Bhairavi* is serene and is to be sung at dawn in a particular *tala.* A *raga* when set to *tala* is pleasing and has an emotional appeal.

Inspired by the human-like qualities of *ragas* and *raginis,* excellent paintings called *ragamala* miniatures were created by the Rajputs.

Who are known as the 'Trimurti' of Carnatic music?

Three great saint composers – Thyagaraja, Muthuswami Dikshitar and Shyama Sastri are known as the 'Trimurti' of Carnatic music. They were not only contemporaries during the later half of the 18th century and the beginning of the 19th century, but were also, incredibly, born in the same town of Thiruvarur in the Thanjavur district of Tamil Nadu.

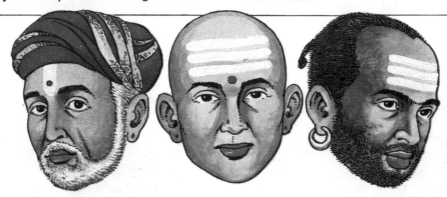

Thyagaraja, a devotee of Lord Rama, was a gifted poet in Telugu and Sanskrit. He composed 24,000 songs, of which 700 are available today. They range from the simplest lyrics to extremely complex masterpieces. So versatile was he that even when he composed 30 songs in the same *raga,* no two songs were alike !

Dikshitar was a learned composer who wrote scholarly songs in Sanskrit. Out of his 400 compositions, some are in Hindustani *ragas.*

Shyama Sastri was the youngest of the three and less than 50 of his compositions are extant. His compositions highlight rhythmic intricacies.

There is a saying in south India that the sweetness of Thyagaraja's music can be enjoyed straightaway like grapes; that of Sastri's like the banana which needs only a quick peeling; while to relish Dikshitar's music involves the effort of cracking a hard coconut before one can savour the sweetness of the kernel !

Thyagaraja's death anniversary is observed as an *aradhana* every January in Thiruvarur, where the world's largest musical festival is held.

What are the earliest musical instruments?

Hunting tools, rods and sticks, pots and pans, in fact, anything from which sound could be elicited by striking, became the first musical instruments. Of these two instruments have become popular – the *Ghatam* and the *Jaltarang*.

The *Ghatam* which literally means an earthern pot with a narrow mouth and a big belly, is one of the most ancient percussion instruments. It is played both in south India and Kashmir.

In south India, the *Ghatam* is held with its mouth resting on the bare belly of the player who taps its surface with his fingers. An expert player of the Ghatam can easily produce a variety of sounds.

In Kashmir, the *Ghatam* is called the *Noot* and the singer uses it as an accompaniment to his singing by striking it on the sides and the open mouth of the pot.

The *Jaltarang* meaning 'water waves' has a set of porcelain bowls of different sizes, filled to various levels with water. The player, by arranging the bowls in a semi circle, in front of him, strikes them with thin bamboo sticks.

Who is credited with the invention of the Sitar and the Tabla?

The invention of the sitar is commonly credited to Amir Khusro, a very talented musician, poet and statesman at the court of the Khalji and Tughlak Sultans of Delhi in the 13th century.

The name sitar is derived from the Persian expression *seh-tar* meaning 'three strings', which the instrument originally had. The modern sitar has seven strings. It is possible that Amir Khusro might have improved upon one of the ancient lyres then in vogue which led to the invention of the sitar.

The pair of drums also known as tabla, is believed to be one of the innovations of Amir Khusro. The *pakhawaj*, one of the most ancient of percussion instruments, was cut in the middle, into two. The piece with a narrow mouth, came to be known as tabla and the broad-mouthed one, as the *bayan* or *dugga*. The name 'tabla' seems to have been derived from an Arabian drum called *tab* !

Which are the classical dance forms of India?

There are several highly-developed classical dance forms popular in India.

The oldest is **Bharatanatyam** originating from Tamil Nadu. Until about 200 years ago, it was called Sadir and was performed by *devadasis* in temples. The present themes and musical content of Bharatanatyam were written and composed by the musicians of the Tanjore court. It is danced to the accompaniment of carnatic music played on *mridanga, veena,* flute and cymbals.

Mohini Attam, meaning 'the dance of the enchantress', originated in Kerala. It resembles Bharatanatyam and was evolved during the reign of Maharaja Swati Tirunal of Travancore (Kerala) in the early 19th century. He composed most of its songs. It is a highly feminine dance form, full of beauty and grace.

Kerala is also the home of **Kathakali** which means a story-play. This dance-drama is highly colourful with elaborate make-up and flamboyant costumes. The Kathakali actor has extraordinary control and expertise in conveying emotion through eyes. The dance is an all-night performance in which the actors enact the story sung by the musicians.

The **Kathak** dance form has nothing in common with Kathakali. Originally *kathaka* was a story-teller who, while narrating stories from the epics employed some gestures and movements to enliven the story. Later, these simple actions acquired a definite form and evolved into an expressive art of dance and mime. It flourished under the patronage of Nawab Wajid-Ali Shah of Lucknow. A distinguishing feature of Kathak is the spinning or brilliant cyclonic turns which a dancer executes in a dance sequence. The *tablas* and the *sarangi* are necessary accompaniments for a Kathak dancer.

The **Odissi** dance takes its name from the state of Orissa. Although mentioned in the *Natya Shastra,* this dance form has only been revived in the last 40 years. Originally, it was danced by Maharis (*devadasis*) in the Jagannath Temple. Later Odissi dancing became restricted to boys who, dressed as girls, performed it during festivals. Today, this dance form is gaining great popularity. Jayadeva's Sanskrit poem, *Gita Govinda* has been choreographed in this dance form.

The **Manipuri** dance derives its name from Manipur, the 'jewelled state' in the north east of India. The *Raslila* of Lord Krishna in Manipuri style is unique. In this dance, the whole body is used to give expression to various moods. The dazzling costumes of mirrored skirts and gossamer veils enhance the charm of this dance, while the *mridang* and *eartaal* form an integral part.

Why is God Shiva revered as Nataraja, Lord of the Dance?

God Shiva is believed to have devised the entire basic vocabulary of the classical dance. He is said to have created 108 different dances, some calm and gentle, others robust and fierce. Of the fierce type, the most famous is the *Tandava*. Shiva is said to have danced 64 kinds of *Tandavas* and there are references in literature recounting where and why he performed them. The *Tandava* dance of Shiva has found wide representation in sculpture and iconography. The temples of Brihadeshwara and Chidambaram in Tamil Nadu have 108 dance poses of Shiva sculpted in the walls. The magnificent bronzes of Shiva as Nataraja representing his cosmic *lila* (play) are considered the greatest masterpieces of Indian art.

What was the oldest form of folk entertainment?

A puppet show was perhaps the oldest form of folk entertainment. Puppetry itself was a folk art and puppeteers were traditionally travelling entertainers, wandering from village to village with their dolls. Usually stories from history and mythology were portrayed and a skilful puppeteer could make the puppets enact any human feat. Puppets are manipulated in five ways: through string, glove, rod, shadow and marionettes. String puppets, popularly called *Kathputlis*, are the oldest, and mostly used in Rajasthan. The glove or hand puppet is worn like a glove on the operator's hand and manipulated. These are popular in Madras and Kerala. The rod puppet in vogue in Bengal, is held aloft on a rod. Shadow puppets are flat cut-out figures atop a rod wire and set against a transparent illuminated screen. Such puppets are seen in Kerala, Karnataka, Andhra Pradesh and Orissa. The marionette is a puppet with any number of moving parts controlled by strings suspended from a controlling rod held by the puppeteer.

Puppetry lost its popularity with the advent of radio, cinema and television. Fortunately, it is now being revived for entertainment and educational purposes.

Where does the traditional form of Sanskrit theatre exist?

Kerala's Kudiyattam is the only surviving tradition of Sanskrit theatre found in India.

Drama in ancient India was accompanied by music and mime. The *Natya Shastra,* a treatise on the art of drama, written some 2,000 years ago, lays down principles that govern these arts including the architecture of the theatre. Interestingly, a ruined cave at Ramgarh in the Vindya Hills of Madhya Pradesh fits with the general description of theatres given in the *Natya Shastra.*

Kudiyattam, which literally, means 'joint acting', involves several actors. The process of acting is so elaborate that a performance of only one act of a five-act play, takes up five or six evenings. Visually, the actor looks similar to a Kathakali dancer. The play is performed in a specially designed theatre in a temple compound so that the actors may face the deity. Kudiyattam as an art form is facing extinction with very few existing performers.

What is Chhau?

The **Chhau** is a folk dance, its name derived either from *chhauni* (a military camp) or from the word *chhaya* (shade or mask).

The Chhau is danced in three states of India – Seraikella in Bihar, Mayurbhanj in Orissa and Purulia in West Bengal. But each state has its own style. The Mayurbhanj style does not use masks, while the other two use masks made of paper, cloth and clay. The dancers are only men. All three styles probably have a common origin rooted in the martial arts tradition and the rich regional culture.

Earlier, the royal families of Seraikella and Mayurbhanj were intimately associated with Chhau. The Chaitra festival, during which the dance was performed, was celebrated in their palaces. Today the festival is organised by the state governments. Chhau today is a dying art.

What is Jatra?

Jatra is the folk theatre of Bengal. Around the 15th century, when the Bhakti movement swept Bengal, devotees went singing and dancing in processions, narrating the events of their god's life. This collective singing amidst the clang of gongs sent some singers into an ecstatic trance. This singing with dramatic elements gradually came to be known as 'Jatra', which means 'to go in a procession'.

At first, Jatra was performed in temple courtyards. Now it is staged. Troupes have been formed and new themes such as historical romances, lives of saints and social reformers and political events, have been added. Still it retains its musical character. When a Bengali goes to see a performance he says that he 'will sing' a Jatra. And the actor who delivers the lines in prose says that he is going 'to sing' a Jatra ! During the Durga Puja festival, Jatra competitions are held.

Nautanki, Ramlila and Raslila are forms of folk theatre of north India. It is called Bhavai in Gujarat; Tamasha in Maharashtra; Therukoothu in Tamil Nadu and Yakhagana in Karnataka. These theatre forms delineate glimpses of the rich folk culture of India.

Where did man first draw or paint pictures?

Pictures drawn on rock surfaces have been discovered in caves at Bhimbetka near Bhopal in Madhya Pradesh. Over 10,000 years ago, man sought shelter

here from the dark nights and preying beasts. Pictures of animals that he feared, fought and killed, fired his imagination and found expression in drawings. Some of the animals depicted, such as rhinoceroses are now extinct in this part. There are pictures of hunters with bow and arrow in hand, swinging to a vigorous dance. Not only were pictures drawn, they were also painted in red dust mixed with melted animal fat. These 'rock paintings' discovered in the 19th century, are evocative and interesting.

What are 'miniature paintings'?

A 'miniature painting' is a small painting executed with great detail. The word 'miniature' was first used to describe small pictures adorning the margins of pages of books. One of the colours used in painting these pictures was red obtained from red-lead, called 'minium'. The word 'miniature' was taken from this.

and Krishna, the seasons in all their glory, and the daily lives of the common people. Their speciality, however, was the introduction of beautiful landscapes as the background in the pictures. *Ragamala* miniatures expressing the emotional content of musical melodies, come under this style of painting.

Indian miniatures are mainly of the Mughal and Rajput styles. The Mughals, being great patrons of art, invited painters from Persia to work with Indian artists. The vibrant blending of their styles created the Mughal style of miniatures. The main theme of these paintings was court life. Others included potraits of royal personages, hunting scenes and drawings of rare birds, animals and flowers.

The Rajput paintings are associated with the Rajputs of Rajasthan and the hill Rajputs of Punjab. Their themes include incidents from the lives of Rama

HANDICRAFTS

How ancient is silk weaving ?

Silk was in use long before the age of the epics. In the *Ramayana,* it is mentioned that among the wedding gifts of Sita, there were 'fine silken garments of different colours'. Silk was exported even to Europe and Persia.

Many of the legends woven around silk claim that sericulture (the raising of silkworms) began in China in 2640 B.C. and was a zealously guarded art. The export of silkworm eggs was punishable by death. It is believed that the Buddhist monks hid the silkworm egg and the seeds of the mulberry trees and later smuggled them to India. Whatever may be the legend, India had developed both sericulture and silk weaving independently by 2000 B.C.

In the centuries that followed, weaving of silk became closely allied to religious observances and rituals. Thus the two greatest centres of silk weaving developed in the ancient temple cities of Varanasi (Benaras of old), and Kanchipuram, to meet the needs of the temple rituals and the demands of visiting pilgrims. Today, these temple towns are known throughout the country and indeed the world over, for the splendour of their handwoven silks. Another incentive to silk weaving was royal patronage, which helped the enlarge their sphere and develop new skills. At present, India produces a variety

What is Tussar ?

Tussar is one of the four varieties of silk produced in India – the other three being mulberry, *muga* and *endi.* India is the only country in the world producing all the four known types of silk.

Tussar silk is produced from the cacoons of the *tussar* worms fed on oak leaves. Bihar, Orissa and Madhya Pradesh produce the *tussar* variety which is rough and resembles the bark of a tree. Assam produces gold coloured *muga* and rough yellow *endi* from the eri worm, fed on castor leaves. The mulberry silk, as the name suggests, comes from the cacoons fed on mulberry leaves. Mulberry silk is considered to be the finest, and therefore rearing of silkworms for weaving of silk has become an important industry in all the southern

states of India where mulberry cultivation is increasing.

The two greatest centres of silk weaving are Benaras (Varanasi) in the north and Kanchipuram in the south. If Benaras is famous for its brocades in gold and silver, the *tanchoi* silks and *jamdanis,*

the Kanchipuram weaver takes pride in the thickness, longevity and the dazzling colour combinations of his product.

Today, India is the second largest producer of silk next to China and is renowned the world over for the beauty and excellence of its handwoven silks.

Which style of embroidery is named after the *mochis,* the cobbler artisans ?

More than any other state of India, Gujarat has a rich tradition of folk embroidery. The Kutch region, particularly renowned all over India for its embroidered articles, has a style of embroidery prefected by artisans who were once cobblers by profession. Interestingly, while doing embroidery, a fine, hooked awl, similar to the cobbler's awl, is used. Hence the name.

Under the patronage of the rulers of Bhuj, exquisite wall-hangings and door decorations in silk were produced in the Mochi style of embroidery. Sometimes small mirrors were added to the work to lend a touch of glamour. The art passed down from one generation to another and embroidered garments with heavy mirror-work became popular. Women

became very skilful at this craft. Now embroidered garments and other articles with mirror-work form an important part of a Kutchi bridal trousseau.

Which plant has been described as the 'wool bearing tree'?

The cotton plant of India was described as the 'wool bearing tree' by King Assurbaniphal of Assyria (668-626 B.C.) in West Asia. He is recorded to have sent for the 'tree' from India in the 6th century B.C.

The Indians were the first in the world to cultivate cotton. They also knew the art of spinning, weaving and dyeing cloth more than 4000 years ago. The discovery of fragments of finely woven, dyed cotton cloth depict the extent to which weaving was perfected by the Harappans when it was unknown in other parts of the world. It is believed that Indian muslins were used for wrapping mummies in ancient Egypt. And the women of ancient Rome were so eager to have this delicate cloth made in India that they were willing to pay any price for it. The Romans even complained that all their gold was being used to buy Indian cloth !

For dyeing, natural dyes such as indigo leaves, tumeric roots, pomegranate skins and lac were used. In fact, India used to export natural indigo to other countries till 1870, when synthetic indigo was developed.

How is Khadi different from handloom?

Before spinning and weaving became mechanised in the 19th century, all textiles were handspun and handwoven. Such cloth, still produced, is now called Khadi, while handwoven fabrics made of mill spun yarn, are called 'handlooms'.

Khadi is intimately connected with Mahatma Gandhi and symbolises India's freedom struggle.

Which ancient techniques of fabric printing are still in use ?

Block printing, tie-and-dye and *kalamkari* printing are ancient styles of designing fabrics, much in vogue even today.

In block printing, designs carved on wooden block are transferred on to the cloth by dipping the block in colours. This process of hand printing is well-known all over India.

From Andhra Pradesh comes the *Kalamkari* style of printing. The word *kalamkari* means 'handiwork by pen or brush'. Designs are first block printed and then painted with a reed pen. The printed areas are later covered with wax and the cloth is dipped into blue dye. After removing the wax in hot water, other colours are painted directly on it.

The unique tie-and-dye methods belongs to the Rajasthan region. It is also called *bandhana,* meaning that which is tied. Parts of the cloth that are not to be dyed, are tied with thread. The whole process, from beginning to end, is fascinating to watch.

The wax technique which has come to be known as batik in many countries, is also widely used.

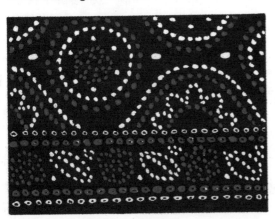

How is the value of a carpet estimated?

The value of a hand-made carpet often depends on the number of knots per square centimetre. The more knots, the more intricate the design and therefore more expensive the carpet. The knots can be as many as 600 per sq. cm. for silk carpets and 300 per sq. cm. for woollen carpets. Most carpets today are double-knotted and have a cotton backing.

Though carpet-weaving originated in Persia, India has taken over as the world's largest manufacturer of oriental carpets. The skilled weavers of Kashmir, Agra and Jaipur can reproduce the classic Persian designs and many original designs, to perfection. A fascinating feature of hand-made carpets is that the colours seem to change when the carpet is viewed from different angles.

Although Kashmiri carpets are generally the most expensive, they are valued as exotic works of art and command a very high price.

What is Kangri?

The Kangri, a quaint device for keeping warm, is unique to Kashmir.

The Kangri is a small wicker-covered clay pot containing a smouldering fire covered with leaves. A wooden or iron spoon is attached to it to stir the fire. It is tucked beneath the *pheran* (loose kurta) worn by both men and women.

Often a handle of woven willow is also added to facilitate holding the Kangri while moving about.

The Kangri is usually plain. The bridal Kangri, however, is very decorative, made from the most superior wicker, dyed in different colours and decorated with mirrors and shiny foil.

This unusual and unique warming pot is one of Kashmir's oldest crafts.

What is Attar?

Attar is fragrant oil or perfume obtained from the petals of flowers, specially roses. *Attars* are also made from other aromatic materials such as *keora, khas, must, hina* and even earth! The *attar* made of earth smells like the fragrance emitted from parched earth on receiving the first shower of rain!

References to perfume are made from the earliest times. An old Indian perfume, spikenard, made from an aromatic plant with rose-purple flowers, was exported to a number of countries including Egypt. Sandalwood paste, however, was the first perfumery material used in India. Emperor Akbar had a special department of perfumery, where experiments were made, day and night, to prepare exciting perfumes. And it is well known that Empress Noor Jahan discovered the *attar* of roses.

In India, *attar* is prepared by distilling the aromatic materials and absorbing the perfumed vapours in sandalwood. Flowers are distilled with about four times their weight in water. They are picked before sunrise to get the highest oil yield.

NOOR-JAHAN

Kannauj and Jaunpur in Uttar Pradesh were once the largest centres of distillation in North India.

What is the origin of handmade paper?

Before the invention of paper, people in India wrote and painted on the long, narrow, dried leaves of the palm tree. Then about 500 years ago, people began to make paper from the pulp of cotton, jute and bamboo. Making paper by hand was quite a complicated process, yet the paper was found suitable for miniature paintings.

Of late, handmade paper has become very popular. Fine cotton rags are used for fine paper and coarse cotton rags for thick coarse paper. One can have golden or silver *zari* paper in any colour, thickness and texture!

The making of handmade paper is a village industry—Rajasthan, Uttar Pradesh, Maharashtra and Tamil Nadu being engaged in this industry. All kinds of wastes such as rags, cotton waste, wood shavings, bagasse, banana stalks, jute husk and silk waste are used in making drawing paper, writing pads and envelopes, albums, greeting cards and fancy decorative paper.

What are Tazias?

Tazias are supposed to be the replicas of the tombs of the martyrs of Karbala. Made of paper and bamboo, *tazias* are taken out during Moharram to mourn the martydom of Hussain, the Prophet's grandson. This religious tradition was initially started by the Mughal emperors.

The *tazia*-maker who specialises in this craft takes nearly a month for the completion of each *tazia*. Depending on the requirement, the *tazia* can have any number of floors – even up to thirty – each floor being marked by intricate *mehrabs* (arches). Once the bamboo frame is ready, it is dressed with cloth and then decorated with delicate paper patterns. Besides the *tazias,* decorated *alams,* the standards of Hussain, are also paraded during Moharram.

The *tazia* makers though muslims, use their craft to make effigies of Ravana during the Dussera festival.

What was the first material used by man for modelling toys?

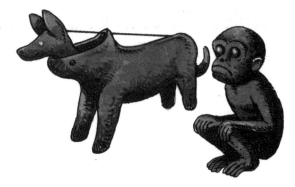

Clay was the first raw material used for modelling toys, being most plentiful, easily available and simple to shape. Toys fashioned in baked clay, for ensuring longer durability, are called terracotta toys. The word terracotta literally means earth red . Archaeologists have discovered terracotta marbles, rattles, a bull with a mobile head and a monkey frisking up and down a string, in the Harappan sites.

Today, though clay continues to be widely used for toys, the other raw materials also utilised are light wood, soft stone, cotton, papiermache, pith, straw, shells and even metal. Although toy-making is a village craft, modern toys excel in workmanship and artistry.

What is the 'lost-wax process' of image-making?

Metals have been used for centuries in India. Archaeologists have found bronze objects made 4,000 years ago by the people of the Harappan culture. The tradition continued through the years because the use of bronze images in worship was preferred. The art of making such images is called the 'lost-wax process' the French word for it being *cire perdue.*

The method of the lost-wax process' is interesting. From a large block of soft wax, the image is carved with its delicate details. Then the complete wax image is covered with clay, leaving just one small opening at the bottom. This mass is first dried and then put into a heated oven. The clay gets baked but the wax inside melts and flows out through the opening. Into this empty mould, molten metal, mainly copper, brass, lead and at times a little gold and silver in certain fixed proportions, is poured and allowed to cool. The mould is then broken open and the metal is given finishing touches. After it is polished, the image is ready for use.

The bronze images of the Buddha made in the 12th century during the reign of the Pala kings of Bengal and Bihar and the Natarajas of Chola kings (11th to 13th century) are the finest examples of this art.

Which metal in its purest form, is described as 24-carat ?

Pure gold is referred to as 24-carat. The term 'carat' signifying the purity of gold has nothing to do with 'carats' used as units of weight for gemstones. As gold in its purest form is soft, it is mixed with other metals and made into an alloy before use.

Gold is one of the earliest metals used by man for personal adornment. Kings used it for their crowns, crests and even thrones.

Popular tradition takes Indian gold jewellery right back to ancient times. In the *Ramayana,* Sita is described as wearing gold ornaments on her forehead, ears, neck, arms, wrists, fingers, waist and ankles. Some of today's neck ornaments and hair jewels owe their origin to the Harappan civilization, 5000 years ago.

Old jewellery design can be seen in the 2000-year-old paintings at Ajanta the Caves in Maharashtra and in the sculptures of south and central India. The art of setting precious stones in gold reached new heights during the Mughal era when *kundan* (gem setting) and *minakari* (enamelling) work became popular. The delicate fairy-like *filigree* work in silver also was much in demand.

Unabated interest in jewellery has kept the standards of this ancient craft as high as ever. The variety is endless. Each region of the country has traditional designs unique to it. There are specific pieces of jewellery worn on different parts of the body. Nose jewellery was possibly introduced by the Muslim conquerors around the 10th century A.D.

ANIMAL
WORLD

Which is the only cat that lives in groups?

Cats are generally solitary, stealthy and wary. However, the only sociable member of this family is the lion that lives in groups called prides. A pride may have one or two mature lions and a number of lionesses with cubs. Members of a pride rest and hunt together.

You will be amazed how duties are so well-defined in a pride. The female is the bread-winner with the male just following the hunting female who makes the kill. But it is the lion who eats first – hence the expression 'the lion's share'! The others sit a few feet away watching. Only after the lion has finished, the next in order begins. The last to eat are the cubs.

Up to the 18th century, the lion's habitat in India stretched all over north India. Today, however, the Gir forest in Gujarat is the only refuge for this majestic animal. The rulers of Junagadh in Saurashtra had declared the Gir forest a reserved area in the beginning of the 19th century and thus saved the lion for India.

Today, one sees the 'king of the forest' usually caged – dozing indolently in zoos or dutifully climbing the high stools at the crack of a ringmaster's whip in a circus – an ignoble fate for a creature who adorns the country's national emblem!

Which animal is worshipped as Dakshin Ray?

It is a general belief in the Sunderbans of Bengal that Dakshin Ray, the creator of honey and wax, wanders in the guise of a tiger, and will not harm those who worship him. Local people, therefore, do not enter the forest without offering prayers to this 'deity'.

The Sunderbans are the world's largest mangrove area. This gigantic forest, named after the precious and useful Sundari trees, is spread over almost the entire Bengal delta of the three great rivers, the Ganga, Brahmaputra and Meghna. In these mangrove forests lives the Indian tiger, also called the 'Royal Bengal Tiger'. Here, one can find the country's largest concentration of tigers.

The Sunderbans are dotted with small villages inhabited by peasants, fishermen, wood-cutters and honey collectors. Before venturing out in to the forests, the villagers offer prayers to Dakshin Ray for the Sunderbans are replete with man-eating tigers. Also, clay models – mannequins dressed as village folks are set up in areas where the incidence of man-eating is high. The dummies are wired to spark off electric shocks to deter tigers from attacking humans in future!

In the Sunderbans, the tiger leads a semi-aquatic life, swimming up to 8 kms from one deltaic island to another. Although game is the tiger's natural food, it eats fish and turtles too. When food is short, the tiger attacks cattle and of course, man. To save both man and the tiger, certain areas have been demarcated as tiger reserves. The Sunderbans is the largest tiger sanctuary in the world.

Which animal's horn consists of substance found in human finger nails?

The Great Indian Rhinoceros is one of the oldest life forms on earth. Its primitive horn is made of tightly packed masses of tough hair, or more scientifically, keratin fibres, the same material from which human finger nails are formed. Actually, a rhino's horn is not really a horn — it is not fixed to the skull like the antlers of a deer or the horns of an ox. Instead, being a secretion from the skin of the nose, it rests in the flesh and can be knocked off by a hard blow. When the horn is thus struck off, the wound bleeds profusely but within a year, a new horn grows again.

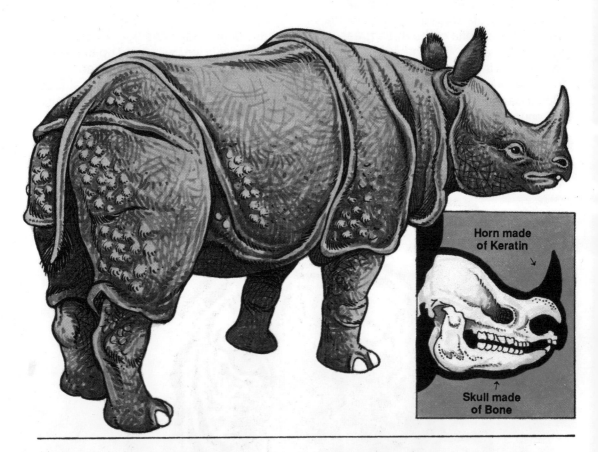

Horn made of Keratin

Skull made of Bone

Superstitions about the magical properties of the rhino's horn have led to the animal's extinction. Ground into powder and made into a potion, the horn has for centuries been in great demand as an aphrodisiac. Kings would keep cups carved out of the horn to test if their drinks were poisoned, for if so, the drink would froth and even split the cup. Consequently, by the turn of the century, a mere dozen rhinos remained in Assam and West Bengal, when at one time, they were found all over the Himalayan foothills.

The Indian rhino is one of the five species found in the world. Unlike the two-horned African rhinos, the three Asian species are smaller and have only one horn.

The Indian rhino lives in the 12 ft high elephant grass in the Kaziranga National Park and Jaldapara Sanctuary in north Bengal. Weighing as much as 2070 kg on a vegetarian diet of grass and water plants, the rhino is the most expensive animal in the world today. In India, a zoo wanting to buy a rhino has to pay about Rs. 1,00,000 for this rare animal!

Which animal is found in the Little Rann of Kutch?

The Indian wild ass, the only wild Asian ass left in the world, lives and breeds in the sandy desert of the Little Rann of Kutch. As one of the world's rarest fauna, the asses have been given full protection since 1952.

Also called *Khur*, the ass is bigger than the local domestic donkey. With short ears like those of the African zebra, it is faster than the horse. When in full gallop, these wild asses move with grace as if they are floating on soft clouds, rather than running on hard saline desert. In the past, a relay of horses were used to tire these animals and eventually catch them.

These asses are quite sturdy and survive without water for a long period, living in herds and feeding during the night and just before dawn. And since their territory has been overrun by domestic livestock, they often wander into cultivated fields. At the slightest hint of danger, they run towards the little islands (*bets*) formed during the monsoon in the Rann, at a speed of 50 to 60 km. per hour.

These swift, tireless coursers, are on the verge of extinction mainly because of the diseases it contacts from domestic livestocks.

Which animal though called a deer is different?

The famous Himalayan Musk Deer, also known as 'Kastura' is a unique deer. It differs from the nine species of deer in India, by having no antlers which other deer grow and shed every year. Instead, the Kastura has tusks!

Some people regard Kastura as an undeveloped deer and place it between the antelope and the deer.

The Musk Deer is a shy, solitary animal living in the upper regions of the Himalayas. The male secretes the prized musk substance from an abdominal gland to remove which, the deer is slaughtered.

The gland or musk pod, when fresh, is not odorous. Only when the outer covering of hair and skin is removed and the gland soaked in water, does the pleasant odour suffuse the air. One single grain of musk can scent over 50,000 cubic m of air! Musk is an important ingredient of several Ayurvedic and Homoeopathic drugs and is also a perfume fixative. In 1973, musk pods were sold for Rs. 6,000 each!

The Government of Himachal Pradesh had established a National Park at Manali for the deer. In Sikkim too, the deer is protected.

Which animal has been saved from extinction by the Bishnois of Marwar?

The Black Buck, the only species of the antelope, is revered by the Bishnois who believe that their ancestors' souls dwell in the Black Buck. Hence they zealously protect the animal and no hunter dares to enter their domain.

The Bishnois derive their name from the twenty-nine – *bis* (20) and *nou* (9) – principles of their 500-year old religion. One of the principles forbids them from felling trees. As a result, every Bishnoi village is a green oasis in the Thar

desert where Black Bucks and Chinkara graze and rest like tame cattle.

For their principles, the Bishnois, however, had to sacrifice many lives. According to a legend, when a Maharaja of Jodhpur sent out loggers to fetch wood for his brick kilns, a Bishnoi woman and her four daughters embraced the trees protesting against their felling. The axes fell and along with the trees, the women were also hacked. Others took their place and 353 Bishnois thus sacrificed their lives.

When the word reached the Maharaja, he stopped the massacre and proclaimed that none of the Bishnois' trees would ever be cut again nor would any of their animals be killed. Later, in 1975, a group of Bishnoi villages, was declared a protected area for the animal.

The Black Buck is one of the most fleet-footed animals and can run more than 40 km. per hour for several kilometres. The Cheetah, which is now extinct in India, was once trained to hunt them.

In the past, herds of several Black Bucks were a common sight. But their numbers have dropped to a dangerously low level due to habitat destruction and poaching.

The male of the species is a magnificent animal with two long spiral horns and a shiny black coat. The doe is hornless and light brown in colour. The beautiful eyes of this animal have inspired poets to use the expression `mrignayani', or 'the one with doe-like eyes'.

Which Indian bird does not fly?

The Great Indian Bustard is a ground bird, heavy in take-off. Weighing around 15 kgs, the bird however, is a swift runner.

At first sight, the bird seems to resemble a small ostrich. In fact, it is a crane-like bird of the open or shrub-dotted plains and its conspicuous white neck is visible from more than a km away. The bird devours insects and grains, and in turn, is itself devoured by man! This bird is quite easy to shoot as it can be approached even in a vehicle.

This spectacular bird undergoes a complete transformation at courtship when the gular sac in its neck inflates to nearly the size of a balloon and hangs between its legs. Strutting before his harem of hens, the bird utters a deep, far-reaching call.

Once a familiar sight in India, thoughtless shooting and habitat destruction has reduced the population of this amazing bird from tens of thousands to just several hundred. Finally, in 1980, it was declared a protected bird in the Desert National Park in Rajasthan.

Which bird is used for mail service by the Indian Police?

In this age of the telephone and wireless, pigeons are still used as carriers of messages and Orissa is the only state of India where the police still have a pigeon mail-service.

Started in 1948, the pigeon post station at Cuttack maintains a loft of about 950 birds. Though the birds annually courier around 5,000 messages to police stations in the hilly terrain, the number of messages double during cyclones and floods when normal communication facilities are disrupted.

Pigeons are found everywhere on earth, except the North and South Poles, being the oldest feathered associates of man. A trained pigeon can fly up to 1000 kms a day and carry a weight of 200 gms. The most amazing thing about a pigeon is his ability to find his way home. How he does it is one of nature's best-kept secrets.

Which crocodile is associated with the River Ganga?

The Gharial. The Ganga is often depicted in sculptures as a beautiful maiden riding on the back of the Gharial.

The Gharial, which lives in rivers, mainly the Ganga and its tributaries, is the sole surviving member of an extinct family of crocodiles. The reptile gets its name because the adult male grows a pot-like knob on the tip of his large snout that looks like an inverted pitcher or *ghada,* hence the name Gharial.

The Gharial often reaches a length of seven metres. The male Gharials are especially sought after for their large size and beautifully sealed hides, which are used in the manufacture of leather goods ranging from shoes to wallets. In 1975, a mere four Gharials were left in the Ganga and a few others were seen in the river system of Uttar Pradesh. Under the Wildlife Protection Act, a total ban on its killing was imposed. Besides, the reptile was bred in captivity for the first time at the Nandankanan Sanctuary in Orissa. Their largest collection is found in the Katarniaghat Crocodile Sanctuary in Uttar Pradesh.

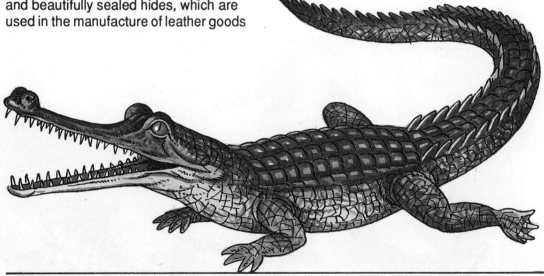

Also, the first Crocodile Bank was founded near Madras in 1976 where the other two Indian crocodiles – the Muggar or the marsh and the estuarine or salt water crocodiles are bred for commercial crocodile farming.

Which poisonous snake is worshipped in India?

Of the over 200 species of snakes in India, only the Cobra is worshipped all over the country.

The King Cobra and the Common Cobra are known by their fan-shaped hood which is formed when the cobra is excited. The venom of the cobra, although not as potent as that of the Krait, is fatal as the Cobra injects a larger dose that acts on the nervous system of the victim.

Yet the deadly Cobras that infect the rice fields of Shirala, a small village near Bombay, are handled almost reverently and fearlessly by the people. Convicted that these reptiles will not strike, the people celebrate the festival of **Nag Panchami** in a unique way.

A few days before the festival, they start trapping Cobras in earthern pots. On the festival day, they remove and display them before the village deity one by one. Holding the tail of the Cobra in one hand and the terrifying head in the other with the poisonous fangs intact. Incredible, but the Cobras do not attempt to strike their handlers! The Cobras are later released.

Which is the only Indian fish to migrate from the sea to the river for breeding?

Hilsa. During the months of July and August, shoals of these fish ascend rivers like the Ganga, Brahmaputra, Godavari, Krishna and Narmada to breed and then return home to the seas and estuaries.

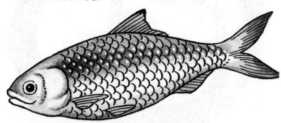

There are three species of Hilsa found in India. One type is found both in the Bay of Bengal and the Arabian Sea but is caught more on the Coromandel coast. Another kind is seen only in the Bay of Bengal. It ascends the estuaries of the Ganga and sometimes goes as far as Allahabad to breed. In Bengal, Hilsa is a very popular food. The third type is common on the Bombay coast. A female Hilsa produces 2,80,000 eggs each season but a large number of them die before hatching.

Where is the Marine National Park located?

A group of about 40 coral islands collectively known as Pirotan Island in the Gulf of Kutch near Okha, Gujarat, form the Marine National Park. Incidentally, it is the first marine park in India formed in 1980 where one can sight marine creatures ranging from colourful sponge colonies, attractive coral heads to large flowerlike sea anemones, crabs and hundreds of varieties of fish. The star performers are undoubtedly the octopii. Highly intelligent, these creatures change colours, squirt dark ink to divert attention and jet off to the smallest of cavities and squeeze into them. Then there are the starfish – which are not fish – and other sea creatures, all colourful, slow moving and more plantlike. Marine snails, cowries and sea slugs together with sharks provide a new dimension to creatures living in the water.

GEOGRAPHY

Which is the oldest mountain in India?

The Aravallis in north western India are the oldest mountain range in India. They were uplifted about 6000 to 7000 millions years ago whereas the Himalayas took 50 to 60 million years to attain their full height! The present Aravallis no longer have its earlier stature when several of its summits nourished glaciers and formed India's main watershed. Long continuous erosion has reduced them significantly.

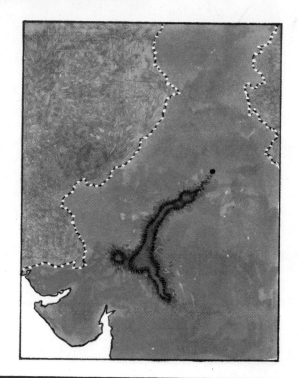

At present, the Aravalli range extends for about 800 kms from Delhi to Ahmedabad. Near Delhi, it is a rocky hillock called the Delhi Range. But the range is most prominent in Rajasthan where it divides the state into two geographical regions. Its highest peak, Gurushikhar, 1722 m high, is on the Abu hills in Rajasthan.

How did the world's highest mountain peak get its western name, Everest?

Initially, mountains are ascribed Roman numerals by surveyors. Accordingly, the Mount Everest was originally given the number XV when its height was first computed in 1852. Three years later, when it was established to be the highest peak in the world, it was named Everest, after the then Surveyor General of India, Sir George Everest. Interestingly, Sir George protested against this, explaining that his name was dificult to pronounce and also could not be accurately written either in Hindi or Persian!

Mount Everest, the highest peak in the Himalayas or the `abode of snow' is 8848 m high and is located on the Tibet-Nepal border. Its first ascent was in 1953 by Sir Edmund Hillary and Tenzing Norgay, after at least eight earlier unsuccessful attempts. In 1984, Bachindri Pal became the first Indian woman to scale this indomitable peak.

Mount Everest holds a powerful, and even fatal, attraction for climbers, luring mountaineers from all over the world.

At which point does the river Bhagirathi take the name of Ganga?

To most of us, the names Bhagirathi and Ganga are synonymous. Yet at the source, the river is known as Bhagirathi. At Deva Prayag in Uttar Pradesh, the river Bhagirathi gets the name, Ganga.

This holy river rises in the snow-capped Himalayas from a little cave, called the Goumukh or cow's-mouth. It emerges as Bhagirathi, named after the royal sage Bhagirath whose penance is believed to have made it descend from heaven to earth. Joined by other streams and after flowing for some 175 kms, the Bhagirathi reaches the hamlet of Deva Prayag. After joining the Alaknanda, it merges into the mighty Ganga. Deva Prayag is therefore one of the holiest of confluences attracting pilgrims from all over India.

Winding through the low foothills of the Garhwal, the Ganga emerges out of the Himalayas near Hardwar. From here starts her densely populated plain which lies in Uttar Pradesh, Bihar and Bengal. The plain owes its richness, fertility, industrial and economic development mostly to this river. Hardwar, Allahabad, Varanasi are the holy cities on its banks. On its lower reach, the Ganga joins the Brahmaputra and the two together form the world's largest delta.

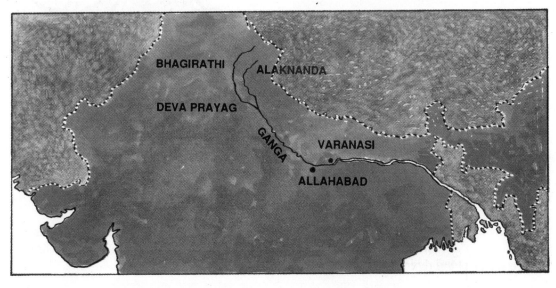

Which is the only Indian river known by a male name?

The Brahmaputra, as evident by its name and behaviour during the monsoon when it swells and overflows causing heavy floods.

Rising from a glacier near Manasarover in Tibet where the river is called Tsang-Po, its assumes the name Brahmaputra as it enters India.

Flowing down through Assam, every monsoon the Brahmaputra rises and ravages the valley. When the water evaporates, the remaining silt acts as a pure natural fertiliser, turning the soil of Assam into gold.

The river is given many names, some feminine, during its course to the sea. It is Jamuna in Bangla Desh, Padma after its confluence with the Ganga and Meghna when it meets the waters of the Bay of Bengal.

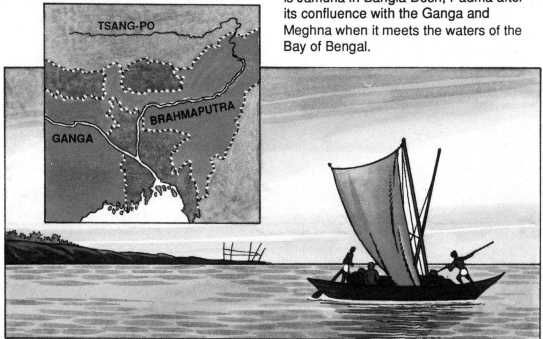

Where does the Salt river flow?

The Luni or Salt River is the only river of the arid plains of Rajasthan. Rising in the Aravallis about 5 kms south-west of Ajmer. The river flows westwards for 450 kms before entering the arid lands of the Rann of Kutch.

The water of the river is sweet at its origin but later turns brackish and by the time, the river reaches its mouth, the water gets quite salty. Hence the name Luni or Salt River.

There are several saline lakes in this arid region of which the Sambhar Lake is the largest.

Which river is glorified as the `Ganga of the South'?

The Kaveri or Cauvery, much revered in the south as the Ganga in the north, is called the `Dakshina Ganga'.

Originating in Kodagu (formerly Coorg) and flowing through the states of Karnataka and Tamil Nadu, the river touches many places of religious and historical importance before merging into the Bay of Bengal. On small islets on the river, thousands of acquatic birds such as storks, herons and egrets breed between June and October.

One spot of scenic allure is where the river has been dammed to form the Krishna Raja Sagar dam, famous for the Brindavan gardens. Beyond the dam, the river divides itself into two branches, encircling the island of Srirangapatnam, the former capital of Tippu Sultan.

Before entering Tamil Nadu, the river rushes into two cascades. The huge volume of water, rolling down the hill and resembling the famous Niagara Falls, was harnessed in 1902 for India's first hydro-electric power project.

At Tamil Nadu, the river splits for the third time to form the island of Srirangam, famous for the Ranganath temple. A few miles downstream is the Grand Anicut dam built in the 11th century and still in use. Here the river separates, once again, into two branches, the Coleroon and the Kaveri. The land lying between these two branches is the Kaveri Delta, the Chola Desa, one of the granaries of India, also the richest in Indian culture, art, music, literature and dance.

The Kaveri joins the sea at Kaveripoompattinam, once a flourishing port known as Puhar or Poompuhar where ships from other countries used to arrive. No wonder, the river is considered the `Mother of the South' for all it bounties.

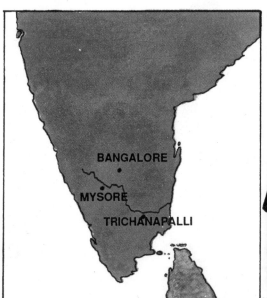

A Kodava couple from Coorg.

Which river is considered the dividing line between the north and the south?

The Narmada, which means loveliness, is the dividing line between the two great cultures of the north and south. Flowing through the states of Madhya Pradesh and Gujarat, the river traces a course of about 1,300 kms before entering the Gulf of Cambay.

Rising on the Amarkantak plateau of the Satpura range, the Narmada meanders to Mandla and turns north towards Jabalpur. At Bheraghat, it forms a magnificent waterfall 15 m high, also known as the Marble Falls, as the bed-rock here is marble with hints of pastel colours.

Of the several holy places on the Narmada, the island of Mandhatta in Madhya Pradesh is renowned for the Onkar temple. The idol is believed to be one of the twelve *jyotirlingas* (original abode of Lord Shiva) in the country.

Emerging from the Rajpipla hills, the Narmada enters Gujarat near Chandod. Meandering through broad curves, the river reaches Broach once famous for its maritime activities and still an important trading centre. Finally the river merges into the ocean near the town of Ambhata.

An unusual feature of this river is its east to west direction of flow. All important rivers of peninsular India flow eastwards. To control the monsoon fury of this wayward river, huge damming schemes in Gujarat and Madhya Pradesh have been proposed.

BHEDAGHAT NEAR JABALPUR

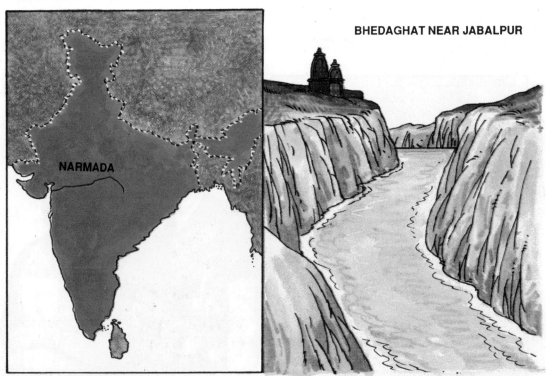

NARMADA

This map does not pertain to be an accurate representation of political boundaries.

Which is the biggest lake in India?

The Chilka lake of Orissa is the biggest estuarine lake in the country. This pear-shaped expanse of water spreading over an area of 1165 sq.km. in the Puri and Ganjam districts of Orissa, is connected through a narrow opening to the Bay of Bengal. The size and water of the lake vary with the seasons: big and sweet during the rainy months as two rivers drain into it; but shrunk and brackish in other months.

Fringed with hills, the lake is dotted with several rocky islands, also the habitat of many kinds of fish and birds. Snakes are found in abundance. Today, unfortunately, the lake has shrunk due to encroachment.

The White-Eyed Pochard, a migrating duck, which comes to the Chilka Lake every year in winter, all the way from Kashmir.

How are the Bay Islands different from the islands in the Arabian Sea?

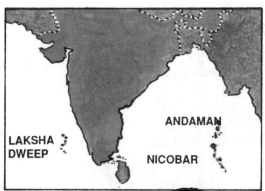

A couple from Nicobar

The Andaman and Nicobar islands, lying in the Bay of Bengal, form India's largest group of islands. They are 346 in number of which 204 are named and only 33 are inhabited. Lakshadweep in the Arabian sea comprises 36 islands, which are small and none more than a couple of kms either way.

The Bay islands represent the elevated parts of ridges rising from the ocean floor. There are, therefore, some volcanic islands too. India's only active volcano which erupted on April 10, 1991, after a gap of two centuries, was on Barren island. The Lakshadweep group of islands, on the other hand are entirely built of corals! These small marine creatures must have quietly worked for over millions of generations to build these islands.

What is the most puzzling seasonal phenomena known to man?

As far back as 326 B.C., Indians and Arabs knew about the seasonal winds of the Arabian sea blowing for about six months from the south-west and another six months from the north-east. The Arabs called them *mausim* (season) from which the English word monsoon is derived. Today, meteorologists describe the monsoon as any wind that blows from a certain direction during one season and from another direction for the rest of the year.

To most of us, monsoon is synonymous with rains. At the beginning of June, the moisture-laden winds burst on the Indian coast of Kerala with thunder and lightning. Gradually, extending northwards and spreading over most of India, by mid-September, these winds retreat and finally leave India by November. For the Coromandel coast, October and November are often the rainiest months. The direction of these winds is controlled by the topography of the country. It is to this seasonal rhythm of the monsoon winds, that the agricultural activity and the life of the Indian people have been revolving over the ages.

Erratic in behaviour, these winds may come early or be delayed considerably. They have caused floods at one place, and drought at another. Unpredictable through the ages, it could be years before scientists understand the phenomenon of these winds.

TREES
AND
PLANTS

Which is India's national flower?

The lotus. A symbol of beauty, purity and divinity, its large fragrant flowers are usually white or pink, though blue and deep rose varieties have been developed.

The lotus basks in sunshine and warmth. In winter therefore, it withers away. Then its roots, which grow in the thick mud at the bottom of ponds and lakes, are pulled out and cooked in a variety of ways. The seed is both a delicacy and an important medicinal ingredient.

The lotus is associated with Lakshmi, the Indian goddess of wealth and prosperity. To the Buddhists, the lotus symbolises Buddha's birth. According to a legend, when as a child, he first took seven steps, lotus flowers sprang from each footprint. *Om mani padma hum* is the Buddhist incantation.

Though the lotus has been extolled in Indian literature and figures in paintings and sculptures of many ages, its real beauty lies in the exquisite living flower.

Which flower has 'threads of gold'?

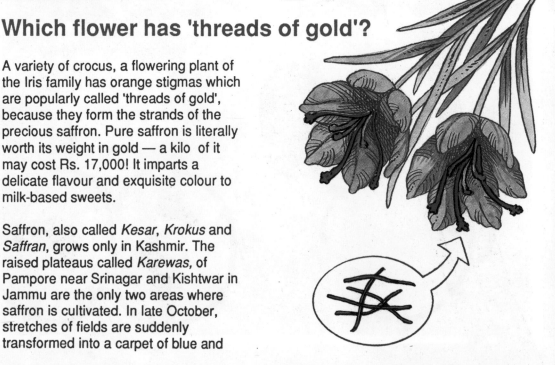

A variety of crocus, a flowering plant of the Iris family has orange stigmas which are popularly called 'threads of gold', because they form the strands of the precious saffron. Pure saffron is literally worth its weight in gold — a kilo of it may cost Rs. 17,000! It imparts a delicate flavour and exquisite colour to milk-based sweets.

Saffron, also called *Kesar, Krokus* and *Saffran*, grows only in Kashmir. The raised plateaus called *Karewas,* of Pampore near Srinagar and Kishtwar in Jammu are the only two areas where saffron is cultivated. In late October, stretches of fields are suddenly transformed into a carpet of blue and gold flowers. But the flowering lasts only two weeks. After picking the flowers, the delicate task of plucking out the golden strands of saffron from within each flower is done meticulously. These strands after being dried in the sun constitute the *Shahi Zaffran*, the finest, purest and most expensive saffron. The rest of the flower parts go to make up inferior grades, which are used to adulterate the better variety.

Pure saffron, it is said, can colour and flavour 700,000 times its weight in liquid and only a few strands are needed for lending an incredible aroma and colour to culinary delights. Saffron is used in rituals and is considered to have medicinal properties. Kashmiris use it in their *kahwa*, the exotic tea they drink. The robes of both Hindu and Buddhists priests were once dyed with saffron.

Which insect directs other insects to the food source by dancing?

Honeybees are highly social. They work together to build a hive, care for their young and gather food. To facilitate the food gathering function, the bees have evolved a 'dance language' a phenomenon discovered by Karl Frisch which won him a Nobel Prize in 1973. According to his amazing discovery, when a worker bee finds flowers ready to yield nectar, it returns to the hive to inform the others. There it describes the direction and distance of the food source by animated 'dancing', either round and round or in the form of figure eight. This coded message includes the whereabouts and the nature of the food.

Honey is one of the nature's most miraculous foods. To make a pound of honey, the bees may have to extract nectar from almost 40,000 flowers. And nectar is merely the raw material on which bees work the 'chemical magic' to create honey – something man has failed to achieve so far.

One of the best known varieties of bees, the *Apis indica*, is named after our country. It is the only domesticable bee of India, reared for apiary honey. As bee-keeping is a rural industry, several varieties of honey are produced in India. Honey is a nutritious and wholesome food, also used in many Ayurvedic medicines.

Where in India is pepper offered to the deity?

In the ancient port town of Kodungallur in northern Kerala, there is a temple where the deity is offered pepper instead of flowers!

Incredible as it may seem, this tiny fruit has changed the course of history. It was the quest for pepper that ultimately led to the discovery of new sea routes and continents.

An indigenous product of the Malabar coast, pepper is perhaps the earliest known spice that was exported from India. The Arabs carried on the pepper trade with India till the 15th century. Pepper was then known as 'black gold' in Europe as its weight was valued in gold and not in currency.

The credit for finding the long sea route to India goes to Vasco da Gama, the Portuguese navigator who arrived at Calicut on the Malabar coast in 1498. Calicut and Muziris (the present-day Kodungallur) were then the spice ports of India. With Da Gama's discovery of the sea route, other European powers quickly followed and the pepper trade boomed in India.

Today, the legendary Malabar coast abounds with reminders of the trade, the practice of offering pepper to a diety being one of them.

What is popularly called the 'Queen of Spices'?

India, better known the world over as 'Land of Spices', is the home of more than 70 varieties of spices. Among these, cardamom enjoys the pride of place for its delicate flavour.

There are two types of cardamoms cultivated in India – small and large. Small cardamom is cultivated in Tamil Nadu, Kerala and Karnataka while the large ones are grown in Sikkim, West Bengal and Assam. In India, cardamom is mainly used as a flavouring agent in the preparation of sweets, curries and also tea. However, it also has immense medicinal value. In ancient times, the

aristocracy used to carry little silver boxes filled with small fragrant green cardamoms as they were considered breath-fresheners and an antacid.

In Kerala, it is believed that a cardamom bush responds only to the delicate touch of a woman. Hence only women pick the pods or capsules. And, have you heard of the Cardamon Hills? Well, that is where this exotic spice is grown in Kerala.

Which leaf gives pleasure to the palate?

Paan (betel leaf) also known as *tambola* and *bira* is an integral part of Indian culture. The chewing of *paan* is widespread and permeates every section of society. Some chew *paan* constantly throughout the day while others do so after every meal. Owing to its enormous appeal to the palate, the *paanwala* is a most familiar sight even in little towns and villages. Smearing green betel leaf with lime paste and catechu, the *paanwala* adds chopped dry betel nuts, dry fruits, sweet coconut shavings and rose paste among other exotic ingredients before folding it elegantly into a tricone and passing on to the customer.

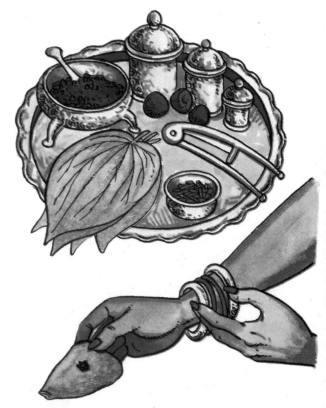

There are *paans* to pander to every taste. The South Indian prefers the plain leaf garnished with shredded coconut. On the other hand, the Lucknawi *paan* may contain a dozen ingredients. Although there are more than 35 varieties of betel leaf available, four are most popular – Poona, Benarsi, Calcutta and Maghai.

The habit of chewing *paan* may have been introduced to India from south-east Asia, but it acquired style and finesse with Muslim influence. A whole cult of social behaviour and etiquette developed round it. Ornate *paandans* (betal box) and elegant spittoons designed in numerous shapes and sizes formed important accessories that went with the leisurely habit of id *paan* chewing. Even the preparation of *paan* was a carefully cultivated accomplishment.

Paan is a symbol of goodwill and friendship and plays a significant role in the social and religious life of the people of India.

Which wood is the most highly valued of all timbers ?

Among India's exotic hardwoods including teak and rosewood, sandalwood is, without doubt, the most valuable. It is valued not only for its inherent qualities but also because it requires special conditions, soil and climate for its growth. Ninety per cent of the sandalwood in India is grown in the two southern states of Karnataka and Tamil Nadu.

This evergreen tree has a life span of about 80 years. The live tree is never cut down for its wood, only the dead ones are uprooted. Moreover, since the tree has a slim bole, the wood is not in the form of logs but of billets.

Oddly enough, sandalwood oil or santalol is a waste product which is stored in the dead cells of its heartwood and in its vast network of roots. The fragrance remains locked up until somebody uproots the tree. Which is why, the tree is not felled but uprooted by a trained elephant. Generally 30 or 40 year old trees are uprooted. All sandal trees are state property by law.

Sandalwood is one of the finest woods for carving and is considered next only to ivory for intricate workmanship. Sandal-carved articles command very high prices. Garlands of sandalwood strips and shavings are used to honour guests; sandal paste, joss sticks and slivers of sandalwood are used both by the Hindus and Parsees in religious ceremonies. Its most valuable product is the oil, which is used in perfumery.

No wonder, a wood so highly prized and priced attracts poachers, who conceal the telltale fragrance of the wood with fish, onions and even garbage to pass checkpoints.

Which state of India is named after a fruit ?

The name `Kerala' is believed to have derived from the word *Kera* meaning coconut. Rightly known as the land of coconuts, Kerala is India's biggest grower of coconuts. The state basks in the untrimmed splendour of its tall, slender palms, reaching to the sky in green grandeur.

The coconut tree grows to a height of 25 m and lives up to 100 years. Once it starts bearing fruit, the tree continues to give a return of about 100 coconuts every year.

The Keralites call the coconut palm the *Kalpavriksha* – the Tree of Heaven or the Wish Tree for every part of the tree is put to some use. The trunk is used to build houses and fronds are matted to thatch roofs; coir is produced from the outer husk of the coconut; the shell is used for a variety of handicrafts; the fresh kernal is widely used in cooking and oil is extracted from the dried kernal, called *copra*. The coconut water is a refreshing drink, containing minerals and used as a substitute for glucose. The sweet water of tender coconuts can also be administered as an intravenous injection!

The coconut is indispensable to most Hindu ceremonies. While launching a ship, a coconut is broken instead of smashing a bottle of champagne! Coconut Day is celebrated to mark the end of monsoon. On Palm Sunday, the Keralites take coconut palm leaves to the Church to be carried home later, as blessed symbols of the Saviour.

Apart from soap, coconut oil serves in the manufacture of a wide range of cosmetics. It is said that the secret of a wrinkle-free face of an aged Keralite is due to the amazing coconut-oil massage done regularly.

What was called 'the choicest fruit of Hindustan' by Babar, the first Mughal Emperor of India?

The Mango has always been acknowledged as the `King of Indian fruits'. Not only Babar, but all other Mughal emperors were extremely fond of this luscious fruit. Akbar, the Great, had mango groves laid out in different parts of his empire. The one at Darbhanga in Bihar had one hundred thousand mango trees, and was known as Lakh Bagh. Even the English and the Portuguese were held under the spell of this irresistible fruit.

The mango tree is indigenous to India and can still be seen growing wild in Assam. Mango groves were commercially cultivated from as early as the time of the Buddha. Now, about 1,400 varieties have been evolved, varying in fragrance, colours and flavours. The growers give them fancy names. Under ideal conditions, the tree assumes enormous proportions. In a village near Chandigarh, the trunk of a mango tree is 9.75 m with about 24 m long branches. It yields nearly 37,000 kgs of mangoes in one season!

The mango fruit is incomparable in variety and flavour. The juicy sucking varieties are consumed in large quantities. Nobody would desire to eat a dozen apples in one sitting, but a mango-lover will gladly forego a meal for this mouth-watering fruit. Mango pickles and chutneys are greatly relished by all.

The mango has been immortalised in paintings and sculptures. Mango leaves are auspicious motifs for religious and social occasions.

Which grass is used for making bridges?

Believe it or not, but a type of grass called the bamboo is strong enough to be used in bridge-making. The Monpas of Arunachal Pradesh make suspension bridges with this miracle grass.

Bamboo grows extensively in the north-east and in the Western ghats of India. In fact, India's natural resources of bamboo is the largest in the world. More than 100 species, ranging from the giant 30 to 40 m tall variety to the one m high, are found in the country.

Bamboo is the world's fastest growing grass – the growth in some species is almost three cms per hour! Many species flower at intervals of 40, 50 or even 120 years, others bloom only once, then wilt.

Though more than half the bamboo produced in India is turned into paper, bamboo has other uses too. A variety of products such as bows and arrows, fans, toys, musical instruments, umbrellas and handicrafts are fashioned out of bamboo. In Bihar, bamboo is replacing steel in tubewell pipes as it is cheaper and rust-free. Artificial limbs made out of bamboo are found lighter. It is used for scaffolding in the construction of high-rise buildings and also as a water container! Pickle and stewed bamboo shoots are regarded as delicacies.

Scientists are still trying to find new uses for this grass.

Which was the most widespread environmental movement by people in India?

The Chipko Andolan or Chipko movement was the first organised protest by villagers of the Himalayan foothills of Uttar Pradesh against the commercial forest policy of the State government.

It all began in March 1973 in a small village of the Himalayas, when, armed with government permission, forest contractors arrived to cut down trees for a sports goods factor. The aghast villagers clung to the trees vowing that they would rather die with the tree than see their forests denuded. This was the beginning of the Chipko movement (*chipko* in Hindi means to embrace). Gradually the movement spread to the entire forest region of Tehri Garhwal and has been kept going largely by the hill folk of the region.

The awakening of the village folk was the result of the disastrous floods in 1970 when several villages were washed away. This tragedy enlightened villages to take up cudgels against indiscriminate felling of trees. "Every standing green tree in the Himalayas is a sentry against the fury of the floods and landslides. Trees not only maintain the ecological balance but also give man the five F's - food, fodder, fuel, fertiliser and fibre. If a single tree has to be cut down at all, at least three others should be nurtured in its place", says Sunderlal Bahuguna, the man who has been relentlessly leading the Chipko Andolan movement.

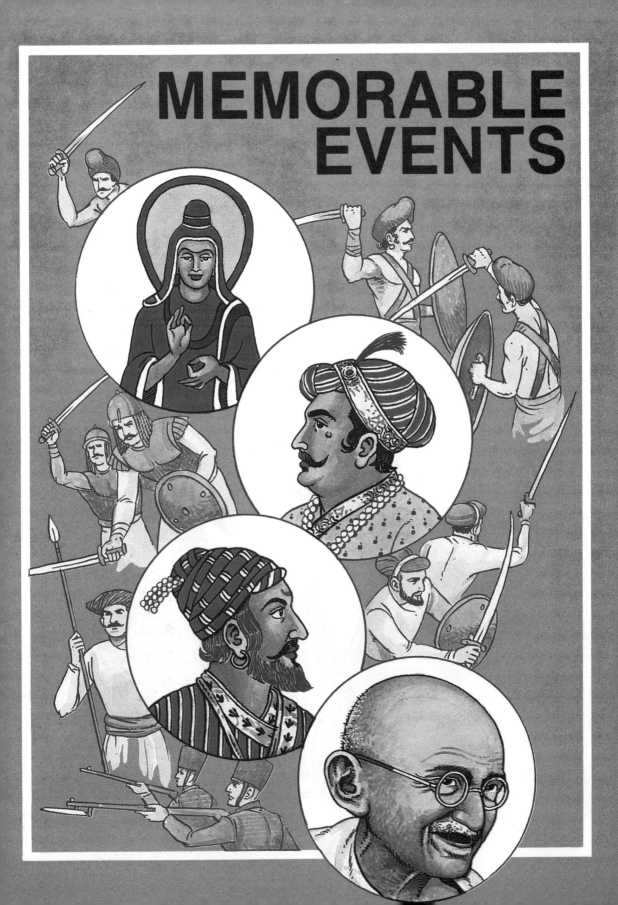

MEMORABLE EVENTS

How is Raja Devanamapiya Piyadassi popularly known in history?

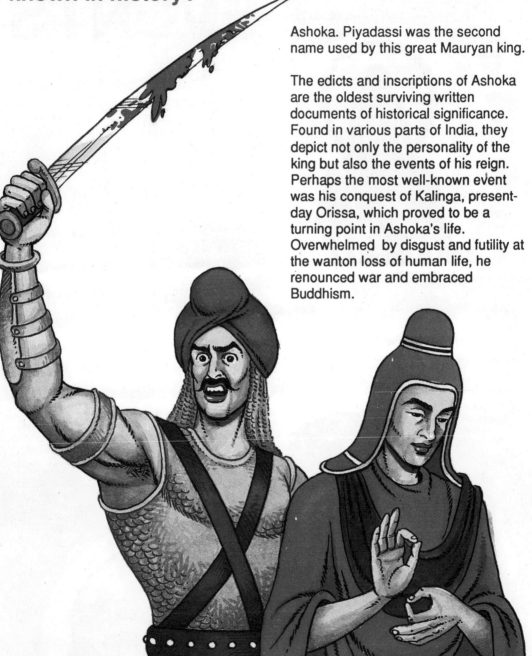

Ashoka. Piyadassi was the second name used by this great Mauryan king.

The edicts and inscriptions of Ashoka are the oldest surviving written documents of historical significance. Found in various parts of India, they depict not only the personality of the king but also the events of his reign. Perhaps the most well-known event was his conquest of Kalinga, present-day Orissa, which proved to be a turning point in Ashoka's life. Overwhelmed by disgust and futility at the wanton loss of human life, he renounced war and embraced Buddhism.

A benevolent king, Ashoka died in 232 B.C. but his memory has been perpetuated by adopting the

Lion Capital erected by him at Sarnath, as the national emblem and seal of free India.

Which was the 'Golden Age' of ancient India?

The period between the 4th to 6th century A.D. when the Gupta dynasty ruled northern India, is often eulogised by historians and travellers as the 'Golden Age' of Indian history. Peace and stability reigned supreme and art and literature blossomed to glorious heights.

The five Gupta rulers, Chandragupta, Samudragupta, Chandragupta II (also known as Vikramaditya), Kumargupta and Skandagupta, at the height of their power, had the Indo-Gangetic plain down to the northern fringes of the Deccan, under their control.

The Sanskrit language reached its perfection in this era. The great poet and dramatist Kalidasa wrote the world-famous *Shakuntala* during this time.

India was more advanced than most nations in science, mathematics, astronomy and medical science. Another significant feature of this period was the growth of important seats of learning. The famous Nalanda University attracted students from all parts of Asia. Many of the splendid rock temples as well as the Ajanta paintings, also belong to this period. The Iron Pillar of Delhi is a living tribute to the Gupta metallurgists, having withstood the elements for 2,000 years without rusting. Even cannon-balls have failed to make more than a dent in its sides. The *Panchatantra* stories delineating animals as human-beings, were written during this period. These stories later inspired the publication of the famous *Aesop's Fables.*

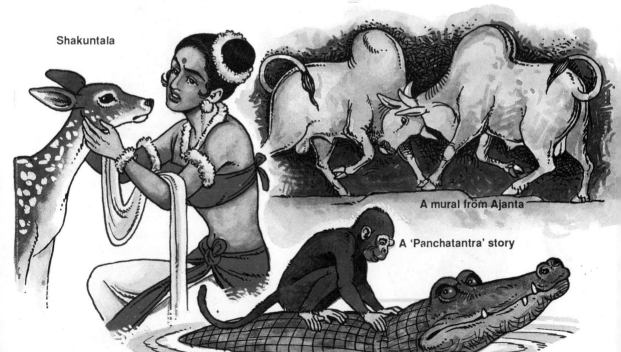

Shakuntala

A mural from Ajanta

A 'Panchatantra' story

But the onslaught of the Huns (Mongols) wrought much destruction to the Gupta empire, and the glory and splendour of the golden age slowly faded away.

Who founded the 'city of victory' in the 14th century?

In the mid-fourteenth century, the Hindu city of Vijayanagar was established on the banks of the Tunghabhadra by two brothers, Harihara and Bukka. Later on, the city lent its name to their kingdom which is renowned in history as the Vijayanagar Empire.

A succession of able kings within a span of fifty years, expanded Vijayanagar to become a major power in the south. The empire reached its zenith during the reign of Krishnadevaraya with unparalled achievements in art, architecture, social organisation and military strength. Travellers, who visited the capital city of Vijayanagar, were overawed by the magnificence of its palaces and temples, its centres of learning and commerce and its firm administration. Canal irrigation was so perfectly planned that the canals are still in use after 400 years!

But when the empire collapsed, the end was sudden and inglorious. In 1665, in the battle of Talikota, five Muslim sultans of the south combined their forces to devastate the kingdom, bringing to an end the Vijayanagar rule. The city was ravaged and destroyed. The monuments which survive, especially the 22 ft high Ugra Narasimha, the family crest, the carvings and murals in the Virupaksha temple, and the stone chariot whose massive stone wheels revolve round the axle, bear testimony to a splendid era.

Which Mughal emperor could neither read nor write?

Akbar, the Great Mughal, never learnt to read. He, however, had an exceptional memory and an enquiring mind which eventually made him a very erudite man. Akbar often stunned scholars by quoting passages from religious texts memorised after they were read out to him.

Akbar was 13 when he inherited the shaky throne at Delhi. Being a man of spirit and strength, he eventually ruled a realm that extended from the Himalayas to the Deccan and from the Persian border to southeast Asia. And, unlike most rulers in that bigoted age, he believed in religious tolerance, laying the foundations of a secular India.

Paradoxically, Akbar had a passionate interest in books which were always read out to him. Of the 24,000 books in his library, the *Hamza Nama,* a tale of heroic exploits, was his favourite. Akbar also set up a department for translating the sacred books of the Hindus, Jains, Parsis and Christians into Persian, the court language. *Akbar Nama,* a book commissioned by him on his reign amplifies text with pictures to facilitate understanding. The Mughal miniature paintings are testimony to that glorious age.

Akbar died in 1605 and lies buried at Sikandra, near Agra.

Who pioneered guerilla warfare in India?

Shivaji, the son of a *jagirdar,* rose to eminence to become a Chhatrapati Maharaj due to his skill in guerilla warfare. He was perhaps one of the first generals in the world to make skilful use of mobile tactics in warfare.

When in his teens, Shivaji captured the hill-fort of Torna belonging to the Bijapur Sultan, by organising the hardy hill-men of the Western Ghats, the Mavlis, into a strong unified fighting force. He continued his exploits till be became a powerful force. How the brave Shivaji slew Afzal Khan and decimated his army, is a pulsating episode of history.

Shivaji's daredevilry did not spare the Mughals whose territories he raided relentlessly. Aurangzeb, the Mughal emperor, sent his armies to tame this 'mountain rat' but for twenty long years, he was unsuccessful. Shivaji excelled in taking the enemy unawares and the Mughals lagged behind while trying to keep pace with Shivaji's fast moving cavalry. Infuriated, Aurangzeb tricked him into visiting Agra and then placed him under house arrest. This visit gave Shivaji an opportunity to perform a daring and dazzling feat – that of escaping in a basket of sweets!

In 1674, Shivaji celebrated his coronation at Raigarh with pomp and assumed the title of 'Chhatrapati'. An enlightened ruler and a great administrator, Shivaji laid the foundation of the Maratha Confederacy. He died in 1680, but is remembered as a symbol of bravery and staunch nationalism.

Which Sikh Guru was martyred in Delhi?

Guru Teg Bahadur was executed at Delhi by the Mughal emperor, Aurangzeb, in 1675 A.D.

Born in Amritsar, the city of the Golden Temple, Teg Bahadur was the ninth Guru of the Sikhs. Sikhism, founded in the beginning of the 15th century by Guru Nanak, propagated the oneness of God and sought to bring together Hindus and Muslims under a common fold. When Nanak died, he left behind a small community who were later called Sikhs. His nine successors moulded the Sikhs into a distinct community with its own language, literature, religious beliefs, traditions and conventions.

When Teg Bahadur became the Guru, Emperor Aurangzeb was the Mughal ruler. Relations between the Sikhs and the Mughals were already strained due to the death by torture of Teg Bahadur's grandfather, Guru Arjun, the 5th Guru, by Emperor Jahangir. The sixth Guru also had a minor clash with emperor Shahjahan. Aurangzeb, a religious zealot, summoned Guru Teg Bahadur to Delhi and ordered him to accept Islam. On his refusal, he was beheaded. His dying message was, "I gave my head but not my faith". This was on November 11, 1675. At the site where the Guru was beheaded, now stands the Sis Ganj Gurudwara at Chandni Chowk, Delhi.

With the martyrdom of Guru Teg Bahadur, the Sikhs finally emerged from being a pacifist sect and turned into a warrior community.

Which episode of India's struggle for independence shook the British empire?

The *Namak Andolan* or the great Salt March was one of the most dramatic and successful episodes of the Indian freedom struggle, eventually changing the course of the country's history.

The British levy on the production of salt sparked off massive protests all over the country. Outraged at the unjust salt tax, Mahatma Gandhi decided to defy government orders by manufacturing salt without paying the tax.

On March 12, 1930, Gandhi set out from Ahmedabad, along with 78 volunteers from Sabarmati Ashram, on a 380 kms trek to the sea-side village of Dandi. En route, the number of protesters swelled to thousands, making the march a sea of human determination. On reaching Dandi, after 24 days, Gandhi picked up a handful of salt, in a symbolic act of defiance. This act heralded a signal to the Indian people to launch a civil disobedience movement by breaking the Salt Law throughout the country. Bewildered by this mass support, the British arrested, imprisoned and beat people. More than 60,000 volunteers were jailed, including Nehru, Gandhi and several other important leaders. Yet the people continued with the struggle doggedly, arousing world attention and appreciation at the courage of the unarmed volunteers. Eventually, the government withdrew the unjust law and the campaign was stopped after 12 months on March 4, 1931.

When and where did Subhas Chandra Bose establish the Provisional Government of free India?

October 21, 1943, was a red letter day in the history of India's freedom movement, as on that day, Subhas Chandra Bose set up the Provisional Government of Free India, in Singapore.

Earlier, in January 1941, Subhas Chandra Bose escaped from house-arrest in Calcutta and went to Japan to fight the British from outside the country. At that time, Germany and Japan were at war with Britain and Subhas Chandra Bose collaborated with them. When Singapore fell to the conquering Japanese forces, Indian soldiers in the British army were imprisoned. Subhas organised them into the Indian National Army or the Azad Hind Fauz with a war cry of *'Chalo Delhi'.*

At a large gathering in Singapore, he proclaimed the setting up of a Provisional Azad Hind Government to fight for India's freedom.

When the Andaman and Nicobar Islands were liberated from the British, in November 1943, the Japanese handed them over to Subhas who renamed them Shaheed and Swaraj Islands respectively. The INA Headquarters was shifted to Rangoon in January. Marching with the war cry of *'Chalo Delhi'* on their lips, the Azad

Hind Fauz, along with the Japanese, crossed the Burmese border and stood on Indian soil on March 18, 1944. How the brave army subsequently advanced up to Kohima and Imphal, how free India's banner was hoisted aloft to the deafening cries of *'Jai Hind'* and *'Netaji Zindabad',* how ironically the atom bombs dropped on Hiroshima and Nagasaki compelled Japan to surrender, and the INA subsequently to retreat, are today part of history.

What is the significance of January 26?

January 26 is a special day for India as on this day, in 1950, the Constitution of India came into force and the country became a republic. Hence this day is celebrated as Republic Day.

The importance of this date goes way back to 1930, when the people of India pledged themselves to regain the independence of their country and observed January 26 as Independence Day.

When freedom was won on August 15,

1947, after decades of relentless non-violent struggle, it was a great achievement. Yet there remained the formidable task of framing free India's Constitution. Indian leaders like Jawaharlal Nehru and Vallabhai Patel, with the help of Dr. B.R. Ambedkar, the first law minister, drafted the rules and laws to govern the country.

Besides the Constitution, the outward manifestations of India's nationhood – its flag, emblem, anthem and calendar were also adopted.

What was Udham Singh's gameplan for revenge of the Jallianwala Bagh massacre at Amritsar?

Udham Singh, a 19-year-old Sikh student was one of the rescuers who rushed to the Bagh after the killing, to render help to the dying and the wounded. What he saw there traumatized him, making him vow to avenge the merciless killing of innocent Indians by the British. He planned to do so by assassinating the Governor of Punjab, an act which was finally accomplished 21 years later!

The Jallianwala massacre took place on April 13, 1919, the day of **Baisakhi,** when thousands of pilgrims gathered at Amritsar to worship at the Golden Temple. It was a prayer-cum-protest meeting against the unjust laws of the British Government. While the meeting was in progress, General R.H. Dyer, along with armed soldiers, entered the enclosed Bagh packed with 20,000 men, women and children. With no warning and without any provocation, his troops fired about 1,650 rounds on a hapless crowd who had no escape route. After ten minutes, when the soldiers had almost expended their ammunition, General Dyer withdrew with his soldiers leaving behind 2,000 people – men, women and children – wounded, dying and dead. Soon after the shooting, curfew was imposed, which prevented aid from being given to the dying. Suspects were flogged in public and in a street, citizens were forced to crawl on their bellies. All this was done under instructions from Sir Michael O'Dwyer, the Governor of Punjab.

Reeling under the ignominy of the Jallianwala Bagh massacre, the British summoned General Dyer to England. After some time, Governor O'Dwyer was also recalled. Udham Sigh followed them to England. On March 13, 1940, he shot dead Sir Michael O'Dwyer at a meeting in London's Caxton Hall, and surrendered to the police. He was later sentenced to death and hanged on June 12, 1940.

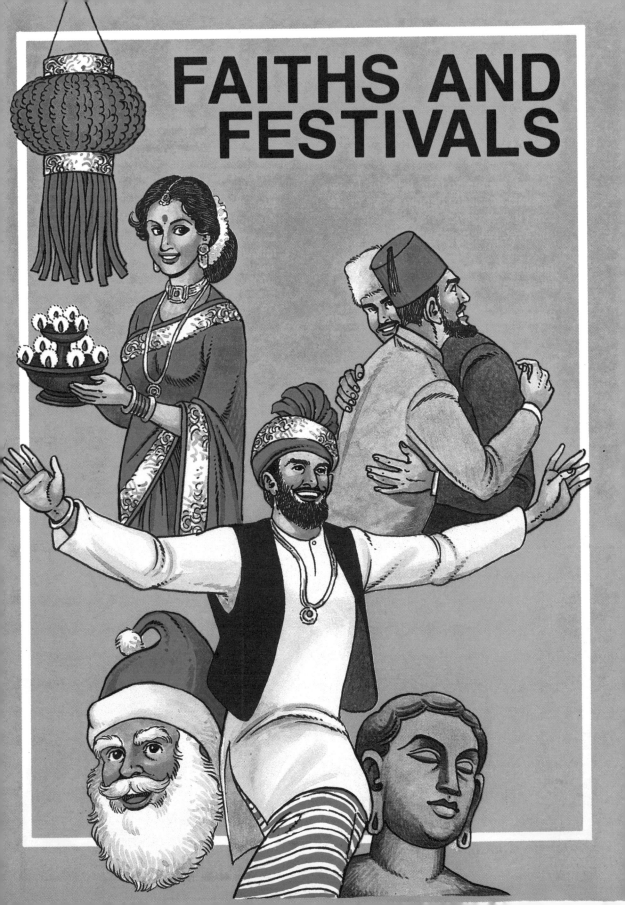

FAITHS AND FESTIVALS

Why is India known as the land of festivals?

The Indian calendar is one long succession of fairs and festivals with almost anytime being festival time!

Though stemming from religion, Indian festivals delineate people's love of life. Even the seasonal changes are observed with pomp and gaiety.

In January, the Tamilians of south India celebrate **Pongal**, a harvest festival.

February and March herald the season of spring and **Holi**, a festival of colours.

The **Id** festival for the Muslims is one of abstinence and thanksgiving.

April brings in **Baisakhi**, the time to bring in the golden wheat, when the farmers dance in joyous abandon as they reap.

With the retreat of the monsoon in August, the festive season starts with **Onam**, the harvest festival of Kerala, followed by **Raksha Bandhan**, a sentimental festival when sisters tie *rakhis*, amulets, on their brothers' wrists as a plea for protection.

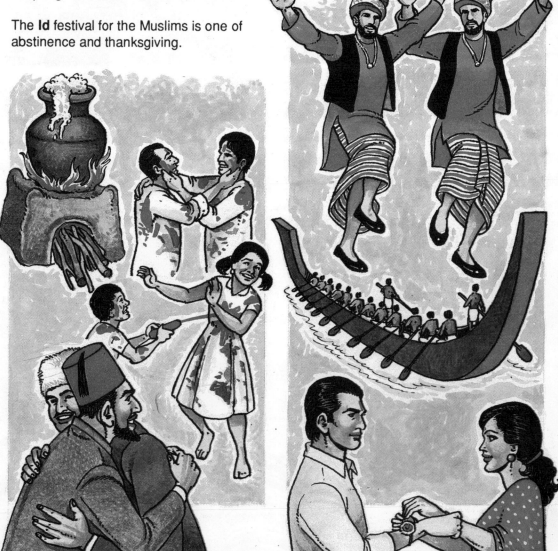

Eight days later comes **Janmashtami** heralding the midnight birth of Lord Krishna.

Ganesh Chaturthi the festival of Ganesha, the elephant-headed God of wisdom and prosperity, is very popular in Maharashtra. This ten-day festival ends with the immersion of hundreds of Ganesha images in the sea.

Before long, it is time for **Durga Puja** or **Dussehra**, a festival celebrating the triumph of good over evil.

Twenty days later, arrives **Diwali**, the spectacular festival of lights, marking the climax of the festive season. Every

Hindu home is cleaned and gaily lit with oil lamps, candles or electric lights, to welcome Lakshmi, the Goddess of wealth and prosperity. Large varieties of sweets are prepared, new clothes purchased and new books of accounts are opened by businessmen.

Around November, the Sikhs celebrate the birthday of Guru Nanak, the founder of their religion, by taking out the *Granth Sahib,* their holy book in processions.

December 25, marks **Christmas,** the birthday of Jesus Christ, celebrated with much revelry and gaiety.

Which are the auspicious symbols and decorations of Indian culture?

Religious symbols are an essential part of Indian culture and the art of sacred symbols has been developed almost to perfection by Hinduism, the oldest living religion in the world.

The symbol *Om* is considered very holy among Hindus who believe that God manifests in the sound *Om*. The word, a compound of three letters a,u and m is therefore used at the beginning and end of a prayer.

All auspicious rites and ceremonies of the Hindu faith also begin with the applying of a vermilion *tilak* topped with a few grains of rice. The hanging of *torana* of mango leaves and flowers over the house doorway on festivals and social occasions too, is an age-old practise.

Another revered symbol is the *swastika* meaning 'well-being', which is drawn at the start of any auspicious work. The account books of some businessmen have the *swastika* mark on the opening page. This mark is especially sacred to the Jains who consider it to be a symbol of salvation.

From the simple design of the *swastika* has evolved *rangoli*, the art of floor-designing with lines and colours. Known in various regions by different names such as *kolam*, *sanjhi*, *alpana*, *mandana* and *athhapu*, the art has flourished in Hindu homes, being passed on from mother to daughter. Entrances of homes and prayer rooms are decorated with these 'good-luck' designs, both floral and geometrical. On festival days and weddings, special designs are drawn. Hindus also represent Gods by *rangoli* motifs.

The medium for these floor patterns varies from region to region. Some use white and coloured powders, while others make designs with rice-flour paste. In Kerala, flower petals are used for designs. Some Parsis use chalk filled into designed stencilled trays to create exquisite patterns.

Which is the most spectacular of all temple festivals?

Although temple festivals are a common feature in India when deities are taken out in procession, the most spectacular and greatest of temple festivals is the **Rath Yatra** or 'Car Festival' of the Jagannath temple at Puri in Orissa. People in tens of thousands flock to this holy town to participate in the world-famous event held every year around July.

Puri, on the east coast of India, is famous for its temple of Jagannath another name of Lord Krishna, who along with his brother Balarama and sister Subhadra, are worshipped at Puri. The **Rath Yatra** commemorates their journey from Gokul to Mathura where it is believed they stayed with their aunt for seven days.

Preparations for the week-long celebrations start several months in advance. On the day of the *yatra*, unusual wooden images of the deities are ceremoniously installed in three huge, ornate chariots which are drawn along a 3 kms. trail with pomp and fervour. Thousands of devotees try to pull the ropes of the chariots in the belief of reaping blessings for this meritorious act. The 3 kms. journey sometimes takes twelve hours to reach its destination! After a week of ceremonial 'holidaying'at Mathura, the deities return to their permanent abode in the Jagannath Temple.

The **Rath Yatra** is almost 800 years old. Every year, at the start of the procession, the Raja of Puri, in a symbolic gesture, sweeps the area in front of the chariots to reiterate man's subservience to God.

Where is the world's largest religious fair held?

The **Kumbh Mela,** a Hindu bathing festival, is the world's greatest religious event attracting lakhs of devotees from all over the country. This festival is held every 12 years by rotation at Allahabad or Prayag where the Ganga converges with the Yamuna and the mythical Saraswati; at Nashik on the banks of the Godavari; at Hardwar on the Ganga, and at Ujjain where the Sipra flows.

The **Kumbh Mela** is as old as the *Vedas*, yet so distinct, myriad and ancient, that it moved Hiuen Tsang, the Chinese traveller, to write extensively about it in his memoirs. He had attended the Allahabad **Kumbh Mela** 1300 years ago as a guest of King Harshavardhana of Kannauj.

According to a legend, gods and demons are said to have shared between them 13 gems that emerged during the churning of the great ocean. The fourteenth, the *kumbh* (pot) of nectar that gives immortality, was taken by the Gods with the demons in hot pursuit. In the flight, a few drops of the nectar fell at the four places where now the **Kumbh Melas** are held. It is believed that a holy dip at these places at an auspicious time, washes away sins and releases one from the cycle of birth and rebirth. This deep-rooted conviction makes the young and old, men and women, sadhus and yogis congregate in lakhs at these revered melas.

Which religion patronises the art of calligraphy?

Throughout the Islamic world, beautiful handwriting or calligraphy, is considered the noblest form of art. As Islam forbids the depiction of images in any form, the copying of the *Quran,* the holy book of the Muslims, was much valued, thus inspiring the art of calligraphy. Calligraphers began copying the *Quran* in exquisite handwriting and gradually developed new patterns in floral and geometrical designs through Quranic inscriptions.

With the coming of Islam to India, new norms in calligraphic art were developed. This art was also used to decorate mosques, minarets, tombs and palaces. The Qutub Minar of the Sultanate period has beautifully inscribed Quranic verses on it.

The Mughals, however, were the greatest patrons of calligraphy, encouraging many new styles in writing. Several books and treatise were copied.

Besides, the designs and motifs based on the Quranic verses were applied as a decorative element to every available medium, such as pottery, tiles, metal, glass, ivory, wood, leather, swords and even armour. The art reached its zenith when Quranic verses were inscribed on marble. The central arch of the Taj Mahal at Agra has letters of Quranic verses so skilfully graduated that they appear equal in size when seen from below.

Where is the tradition of 'looting of the pot' practised?

The 'looting of the pot', a unique practice takes place at the *dargah* or tomb of the Sufi saint, Khwaja Muinuddin Chishti at Ajmer. The *dargah,* the most sacred in India, is considered a wish-fulfilling shrine. On fulfilment of a wish, a devotee offers to get *kheer,* a sweet pudding of rice, milk and sugar, prepared in either of the two massive *degs* (pots). The larger of the two pots, gifted by Emperor Akbar, can hold 4,482 kgs of *kheer* while the smaller one has a capacity of 2,240 kgs!

The cooking of *kheer* starts in the evening. By dawn, the boiling hot *deg* is brought onto a stepped platform where traditional 'looters' dressed in canvas covers, get ready at vantage points. Just after the first prayer, the name of the donor is announced and the cloth over the *deg* is removed. In an instant, the 'looters' plunge their buckets into the *deg* and pass the *kheer* down to their helpers. And when they can no longer draw any more of the *kheer* by buckets they themselves jump into the boiling *deg*. The alacrity with which they work is incredible; in seven to ten minutes the *deg* is scraped to the bottom. The *kheer*, now with the 'looters', is sold as *prasad* to the pilgrims. The event of the 'looting of the pot' remains an indelible experience for the spectators and a topic of animated conversation for days together.

Where in India is the Carnival celebrated?

Goa is the only place in India, and in the whole of Asia, where a Carnival is celebrated once a year, for four days preceding the 40-day period of Lent.

The Carnival introduced by the Portuguese in Goa in 1510, is a festival of the young, starting with the ceremonial procession of King Momo, the Lord of Festivities, along with his queen and courtiers. He is followed by the young in fancy dresses and masks, playing drums and trumpets. The crowds lining the streets shower confetti, lozenges, talcum powder and perfumed water on the revellers. King Momo then commands his subjects to have a good time full of fun and laughter.

Obeying his orders, the whole of Goa goes festive with much frolicking and feasting. Great dances are held vying with each other for the best decor, bands and crowds. There is open air, all night dancing in the streets, squares and even on sandy beaches.

After three days of riotous carnivalling, the jubilation ends, by when, everyone has had enough!

Which three events of Buddha's life are associated with a particular day?

Buddha Purnima, the full-moon day of May, is thrice blessed, marking the birth, enlightenment and *Nirvana* of Gautama Buddha.

These auspicious events, however, occurred at three different places. The Buddha was born in the Lumbini Grove at Kapilavastu near the Nepal border. He attained enlightenment in the Deer Park at Gaya, now called Bodhgaya. *Nirvana* was achieved at Kusinara, modern Kasia in Uttar Pradesh. Yet another site hallowed by the Buddhists

is Sarnath, near Varanasi, where he preached his first sermon and set the 'Wheel of Law' in motion. From here began his mission of non-violence, campassion and humanitarian service. Sarnath became doubly significant as this was the place where the Buddha laid the foundation of his *Sangha* or Order of Monks.

On **Buddha Jayanti**, Buddhists from different parts of the country and from other countries as well, visit places associated with the Buddha's life. Some of these places embellished with monasteries, *viharas* and *stupas* are of historical interest.

Which community celebrates the festival of Hola Mohalla?

The Sikhs celebrate *Holi,* the spring festival, as **Hola Mohalla.** Instead of splashing colours, they observe the day with mock battles, tournaments, parades and displays of martial arts. This unique celebration is mainly held in Anandpur by the Nihangs who take out a procession *(mohalla)* displaying their martial arts.

The Nihangs, baptised by Guru Gobind Singh, the tenth Sikh Guru, as the warrior sect of the Sikhs, are conspicuous by their blue knee-length tunics and blue or yellow turbans, rising to more than a metre high, laced with steel discs. These bearded fighters carry huge spears, daggers and swords.

Every year, lakhs of pilgrims visit Anandpur to participate in the **Hola Mohalla** festival.

Which Jain pilgrimage centre is known the world over for its imposing statue?

Sravanbelgola, a small town in Karnataka, is one of the oldest and holiest of Jain pilgrim centres housing the magnificent statue of Lord Bahubali, popularly known as Gomateshwara. Carved out of a single granite boulder, a thousand years ago, this 17.4 m tall edifice is the tallest monolithic statue in the world, visible even from a distance of 26 kms!

Lord Bahubali was the son of Emperor Rishabhadeva, who later became the first Tirthankara of the Jains. Bahubali had renounced his kingdom after defeating his brother in an epic war, taken to penance, and attained *Nirvana*.

The colossal image of Bahubali or Gomateshwara, is believed to have been carved in 981 A.D. The statue has withstood sun, rain and the ravages of time for more than 1000 years without losing its beauty and majesty.

Sravanbelgola attracts thousands of Jain pilgrims and tourists during the *Mahamastakabhisheka* – the head-anointing ceremony of Lord Bahubali which takes place every 12 or 14 years.

LIST OF
QUESTIONS

ARCHITECTURE

SCIENCE

SPORTS

PERFORMING ARTS

HANDICRAFTS

ANIMAL KINGDOM

GEOGRAPHY

TREES AND PLANTS

MEMORABLE EVENTS

FAITHS AND FESTIVALS